Joana Rita Oliveira Sampaio

VAT - An instrument for shaping behaviour?

Joana Rita Oliveira Sampaio

VAT - An instrument for shaping behaviour?

Implications for Tax Policy

ScienciaScripts

Imprint
Any brand names and product names mentioned in this book are subject to trademark, brand or patent protection and are trademarks or registered trademarks of their respective holders. The use of brand names, product names, common names, trade names, product descriptions etc. even without a particular marking in this work is in no way to be construed to mean that such names may be regarded as unrestricted in respect of trademark and brand protection legislation and could thus be used by anyone.

Cover image: www.ingimage.com

This book is a translation from the original published under ISBN 978-620-2-40762-5.

Publisher:
Sciencia Scripts
is a trademark of
Dodo Books Indian Ocean Ltd. and OmniScriptum S.R.L publishing group

120 High Road, East Finchley, London, N2 9ED, United Kingdom
Str. Armeneasca 28/1, office 1, Chisinau MD-2012, Republic of Moldova, Europe
Printed at: see last page
ISBN: 978-620-8-32424-7

INDICE

1. INTRODUCED

Within the range of taxes that each state has at its disposal and that make up fiscal policy, VAT, as an indirect tax, occupies a pioneering place in taxation, since it is one of the main factors responsible for the largest share of revenue.

Originating in France, where it was first applied, it was adopted by the then European Economic Community. The adoption of this tax within the Community is necessarily linked to the idea of harmonization, since the member states shared different multi-phase and cumulative taxes.

In chapter two (point 2.1) of this study, we will look at the main pieces of legislation that established the tax within the Community, such as the Council Directives of April 11, 67/227/EEC (First Directive) and 67/228/EEC (Second Directive), and Council Directive 77/338/EEC, known as the Sixth Directive, of May 17. The latter repealed the second directive and for almost three decades formed the basis of VAT in the Community, making it an extremely important piece of VAT legislation. We will also mention other instruments (directives and regulations) which, during the period in which the sixth directive was in force, complemented the VAT regulation, among which we highlight Council Directive 2006/112/EC of November 28, commonly known as the VAT directive, which repealed the sixth and first directives. As a result, the "common VAT system" is now contained in a single document.

We will also take a look at the evolution of VAT in Portugal. VAT was adopted in Portugal on January 1, 1986 and replaced the Transaction Tax. The reasons behind the adoption of this new tax were, essentially, the recognition of the merit obtained in the countries that had already adopted it and the growing financing needs of the public sector, which require an increase in tax revenue.

And because our study focuses on the figure of taxation, we can't help but reserve a few thoughts on fiscal policy. After delimiting the concept, we will see that fiscal policy is linked to budgetary policy, which is understood as the process of determining the necessary public expenditure and how to pay for it. The link is justified because the main source of funding for our state and for most countries is undoubtedly taxes.

In this context, and closely related to the subject of our study, we will analyze Law No. 66-A/2012, of December 31[1] , which approved the Major Planning Options for 2013 and Law No. 64-A/2011, of December 30, 2011, which approved the Major Planning Options for 2012-2015. We'll see what changes have been proposed and implemented in terms of VAT, particularly in terms of exemptions and the incidence of reduced rates. We are taking advantage of the *timing of* these changes to take a first look at the objectives of the current imposition of a tax such as VAT. Can this instrument pursue objectives of a different kind, namely to shape economic and social behavior? The context in which we pose this question is somewhat challenging, since the current global economic crisis has required governments to make an extra effort, as they are forced to find strategies to stimulate their economies, in order to get out of recession and achieve some stability. It is this need for stability that has led *politicians to* give economic concerns more prominence than social ones.

Next, we will analyze the VAT rates applicable under Article 18 of the CIVA, listing the goods and services subject to the reduced and intermediate rates, with the exception of the changes introduced in this area in recent years.

Having analyzed the various VAT rates in Portugal, it's time to examine the reasons behind the existence and maintenance of exemptions, zero rates and reduced rates. Whether for reasons of progressivity, fairness or difficulty in taxing, exemptions remain widespread. Among the goods and services subject to exemptions/VAT at zero rates/reduced rates, there are those that are commonly accepted, such as foodstuffs and hospital services, and those that cause some disagreement, such as cultural activities.

---

1 Law no. 66-A/2012, of December 31, page 14 point 2.4.

In an issue where conflicting arguments emerge, there is an almost general harmony in the preference for VAT, especially when the aim of its imposition is to raise revenue. It should be noted that in the three-year period 2010-2012, almost half of the member states increased the standard and/or reduced rate in order to increase their revenue. Only in exceptional cases have some states opted (in some cases temporarily) for a reduction in the tax burden for specific goods and services, moving them to the lowest rates. These changes are justified not only for reasons of distribution (reduced rates for goods such as food or merit goods), but also because of concerns about economic developments in specific sectors such as construction.

Despite the harmony in preference, there is divergence in the tax rate structure. In fact, the different rates implemented in various countries have been identified as a problem that will affect the efficiency of the VAT system, insofar as it introduces complexity, which will result in an increase in costs. It is in this context that arguments for a single VAT rate arise, pointing out that such a structure would, on the one hand, allow for higher revenues and, on the other hand, a reduction in tax costs for the Tax Administration, as well as compliance costs for businesses. In the end, the result could be a lower standard rate.

But why do reduced rates persist? Some positive effects are pointed out, such as the promotion of employment, increased productivity, the promotion of certain goods and products in order to boost cultural awareness or the health of the population and the support of disadvantaged groups.

But which option?

There is no ideal VAT system. The structure and design of such a tax will always depend on the economic, political, social and historical characteristics of the place in question, as well as the level of revenue needed by the public sector to finance the public sector itself. Nevertheless, economic analysis suggests that VAT's greatest potential would be best achieved by broadening the tax base and eliminating reduced rates.

Finally, we will refer to excise duties in a separate chapter, based on the argument that they can be aimed, in addition to revenue, at discouraging the consumption of certain products that are considered harmful. They have therefore been used as a means of influencing consumer behavior in various sectors.

2. HISTORICAL PERSPECTIVE

VAT, as a new and autonomous tax, was first introduced in France by Maurice Laure, then inspector of finance[2] . The context of its birth was the tax reform in that country in 1954 and its aim was to reduce the price of goods. This was because a tax called "production tax" was levied on products. On the basis of this production tax, Maurice Laure created a new tax levied only on the added value of products - value added tax[3] . Given the success of this new tax in that country, the then European Economic Community relented and adopted it at the end of the 1960s, as we shall see *below.*

VAT is currently one of the main sources of revenue in a significant number of countries (more than one hundred and fifty). According to data from the OECD[4] , it accounts for 30% of all revenue collected by governments across the OECD, with VAT being the main form of consumption taxation in 33 of the 34 OECD member states (with the exception of the USA), accounting for two-thirds of total consumption tax revenue .[5]

2.1 IN THE EUROPEAN UNION

In view of the Community objective set out in Article 99[6] of the founding treaty of the European Economic Community of 1957, the Treaty of Rome, to build a common market in order to achieve and guarantee free competition between the member states, the adoption of a tax such as VAT, which has proved successful in

---

2 The concept behind VAT was put forward by the German Wilhelm Von Siemens in the 1920s - see EBRILL V. LIAM, KEEN MICHAEL, BODIN JEAN-PAUL and SUMMERS VICTORIA, The Modern VAT, International Monetary Fund, Washington, D.C., 2001.

3 In the economic definition, "added value" is the difference between a company's sales and its purchases of raw materials and services from other companies. SAMUELSON/NORDHAUS, Economia, copy of the original Economics, 16ª edigao, McGraw Hill de Portugal, Lda., 1999, page 394.

4 OECD (2011), Consumption Tax Trends 2010: VAT/CST and Excise Rates, Trends and Administration Issues, OECD Publishing, page 8.

5 The remaining third is made up of specific consumption taxes, such as excise duties.

6 Article 99 of the Treaty of Rome states that "The Commission shall examine to what extent the laws of the various Member States relating to turnover taxes, excise duties and other indirect taxes, including compensation measures applicable to trade between Member States, may be harmonized in the interests of the common market."

France, seemed to be the right solution. Within the Community, the adoption of a tax such as VAT is necessarily linked to the idea of harmonization. This is because, with the exception of France, which pioneered this tax, the other member states shared multiple and cumulative indirect taxes. Among us, there was a Transaction Tax, the basis of which was the supply of certain goods and services .[7]

The process of implementation and harmonization began with the approval of Council Directives 67/227/EEC (First Directive) and 67/228/EEC (Second Directive) of April 11.

The first directive imposed a deadline for the adoption of VAT in the member states[8] . As the first directive, it contained what were intended to be the general features of the tax then imposed: 1) it was a general consumption tax, levied on transactions in goods and the provision of services[9] ; 2) it was proportional to the price of the goods and services[10] ; 3) it was applied on the output side with deduction of input tax[11] ; 4) it was applied up to and including the retailer stage[12] . This directive also contained the requirement to abolish taxation on imports and reduce it on exports in relation to trade between member states.

As far as the second directive was concerned, it contained the implementing rules of the first directive and, in particular, rules interpreting concepts considered to be key concepts of the new tax, such as the *territory of the country, the tax*able *person, the supply* and *import of goods, the provision of services .[13]*

Despite the definition, as we have seen, of the general terms and measures for applying and implementing the tax, member states were left with a considerable

---

7 Transaction tax will be dealt with, albeit superficially, later in section 2.2 of this study.

8 The initial deadline was January 1, 1970, but it was extended by Council Directives 69/463/EEC of December 9, 71/401/EEC of December 20 and 72/250/EEC of July 4.

9 The directive states that the value added tax system achieves the greatest simplicity and neutrality if the tax is levied as generally as possible and if its scope covers all stages of production and distribution, as well as the service sector.

10 This is regardless of the number of transactions that took place in the process prior to taxation (production and distribution process), see Article 2 of the first directive.

11 Ibid.

12 With regard to the application of the tax to retail trade, the directive states that, since this may cause difficulties for some member states of a practical and political nature, they are left free to apply the common system up to and including the wholesale trade stage, and to apply an autonomous complementary tax to the retail trade stage.

13 See articles 3 to 7 of the second directive.

margin of discretion. Discretion both, for example, with regard to the rates to be applied (only a range between 5% for the minimum rate and 15% for the maximum rate was defined) and with regard to exemptions, since it did not establish an exhaustive list of exemptions to be granted. It should even be noted that, in this last matter, the second directive directed member states to give priority to exemptions to the exclusion of the tax base[14] . From what we have just said, it is easy to conclude that the considerable margin of discretion given to member states could harm the objective of standardization and harmonization[15] , since instead of a common system we could have several (internal) subsystems. If this objective is undermined, it seems to us that the guiding idea of the community - the creation of a common market - will be jeopardized.

Continuing with the VAT system in the European Community, we should mention Council Directive 77/338/EEC, known as the Sixth Directive, of May 17. This repealed the second directive and has been the basis of VAT in the Community for almost three decades, albeit with changes[16] . Important changes include: 1) the introduction of a common list of exemptions[17] ; 2) the obligation to periodically declare transactions carried out[18] ; 3) the harmonization of special schemes and deduction schemes; 4) the clarification of concepts such as taxable person, taxable transaction, supply of services, amounts, chargeable event, among others[19] ; 5) the introduction of a consultation procedure[20] . During its lifetime, the Sixth Directive was complemented by other instruments, such as :[21]

---

14 See Annex A, paragraph 2, second subparagraph of the second directive: "If a Member State wishes not to tax certain activities, it should do so by means of exemptions rather than by excluding from the scope of the tax the persons carrying out the activities in question."

15 Look at the disparity in tax rates, for example at the standard rate, 15% in Luxembourg, 24% in Romania, 25% in countries like Sweden and Denmark and Hungary with the highest rate, 27%. Discretion leads to different treatments for the same goods, depending on the member state. As a practical example, VAT on ebooks in Luxembourg is 3%, while in Portugal it is 23%.

16 There have been more than thirty since its adoption.

17 See Articles 13 to 16 of Title X of the Sixth Directive.

18 Whenever this proves necessary in order to ascertain and monitor the material collectible from own resources.

19 See Articles 3 to 10 of the Sixth Directive.

20 Consultation of member states with a view to drawing up a regular report on the operation of the common system of value added tax in the various states.

21 In addition to those we have specifically addressed, see Council Directive 79/1072/EEC of December 6, Council

- Council Directive 91/680/EEC of December 16 supplementing the common system of value added tax and amending Directive 77/388/EEC with a view to the abolition of fiscal frontiers.

- Council Directive 92/77/EEC of October 19: on tax rates. The motivation for this legislation was the need, felt after the abolition of tax controls at borders and in order to avoid distortions of competition, for a uniform VAT base, but also for a series of rates and rate levels that were sufficiently approximate between member states. In this sense, the 1992 directive amended the sixth directive, establishing minimum tax rates. It established a rate of 15% for the standard rate and 5% for the reduced rate. Alongside this definition, there was also a ban on the adoption of increased rates and, for some member states, (provisional) derogations from the application of the new rates. An annex listed the goods and services to which member states could apply reduced VAT rates .[22]

- Council Directive 2006/112/EC of November 28 (commonly known as the VAT Directive)[23] . This directive repealed the Sixth and First Directives, thus making the *common* VAT *system a* single document[24] . In reading its assumptions, two objectives are revealed as the order of business: on the one hand, the desired harmonization of the VAT system, making it common to all member states, and on the other hand, the control of tax evasion and fraud in relation to this tax. With regard to the former, there is a concern to harmonize the laws of the member states in order to *"eliminate as far as possible any factors which may distort the*

Directive 83/181/EEC of March 28 (eighth directive), Council Directive 86/560/EEC of November 17, Council Regulation (EC) 1777/2005 of October 17.

22 See Annex H of the law in question: list of goods and services to which reduced VAT rates may be applied.

23 Amended by Council Directives 2006/138/EC of December 19, 2006, 2007/75/EC of December 20, 2007, 2008/8/EC of February 12, 2008, 2008/117/EC of December 16, 2008, 2009/47/EC of May 5, 2009, 2009/69/EC of June 25, 2009 and 2009/162/EU of December 22, 2009.

24 This integration of the common system into a single piece of legislation is to be applauded since, among other merits, it facilitates the study, interpretation and application of the tax and its procedure. Subsequent to the VAT directive, see Council Directives 2007/74/EC of December 20 on the exemption of VAT and excise duties levied on goods imported by travelers from third countries; 2008/8/2008 of February 12 which amended the VAT directive on the place of supply of services; 2008/9/EC of February 12 which, among other amendments, defined the arrangements for refunding VAT to taxable persons not established in the member state of refund, took into account the use of new technologies and simplified procedures.

conditions of competition, both at national and Community level"[25] . The pursuit of these two objectives leads to a series of measures and clarifications. For example, with regard to VAT rates, and given the possibility that differences in the standard rates applied by member states[26] could lead to distortions in the Community and, in certain sectors of activity, in competition, a minimum standard rate is set[27] . It also provides for the possibility of derogations from the number and level of rates. In particular with regard to reduced rates[28] , the objectives and effects of maintaining such rates are also questioned. Firstly, it provides for the scope of reduced rates to be reviewed every two years and for an overall assessment report to be drawn up on the impact of applying reduced rates to locally supplied services, including restaurant services, particularly in terms of job creation, economic growth and the proper functioning of the internal market .[2930]

It seems to us that, taking the literal element into account, we can conclude that this figure has some merit, because it provides for member states to be allowed to consider lowering VAT on "labor-intensive" services, as a measure to combat unemployment and, at the same time, as an incentive to give up working in the black economy. However, it does not ignore the risks of a reduction in VAT rates "for the proper functioning of the internal market and for tax neutrality". Therefore, it recommends that this authorization be limited in time and verifiable .[2930313233]

---

25 The taxation of all telecommunications services used in the Community is increased in order to avoid distortions of competition in that field. To the same end, it is provided that radio and television broadcasting services and electronically supplied services from third territories to persons established in the Community or, from the Community, to recipients established in third territories shall be taxed at the place of establishment of the recipient of those services.

26 See Article 96 of Council Directive 2006/112/EC of November 28, 2006 "Member States shall apply a standard rate of VAT fixed by each Member State as a percentage of the taxable amount which shall be identical for the supply of goods and for the supply of services".

27 Article 97 of the same directive states that "from January 1, 2006 until December 31, 2010, the standard rate may not be less than 15%".

28 In accordance with Article 98 of the Directive, member states may apply one or two reduced rates, which apply only to the supply of goods and services in the categories listed in Annex III. It excludes electronically supplied services from the scope of reduced rates (wording introduced by Council Directive 2008/8/EC of February 12, 2008). Article 99 lays down the minimum percentage; reduced rates may not be less than 5%.

29 See Articles 100 and 101.

30 As a result of the amendment introduced by Council Directive 2009/162/EU of December 22, 2009, member states were authorized to apply a reduced rate to supplies of natural gas, electricity or district heating (Article 102). Specifically for Portugal, the directive provides that one of the two reduced rates provided for in Article 98 may be applied to tolls in the Lisbon area, as well as the application of rates lower than those applied on the mainland, to operations carried out in

Of the specific and transitional provisions to which we have referred, we have mentioned the possibility that member states which on January 1, 1991 granted exemptions with the right to deduct VAT paid in the previous stage, or applied reduced rates of less than the minimum of 5%, may maintain them in force and therefore continue to apply them. However, these exemptions or rates must be justified on grounds of social interest and for the benefit of end consumers[32][33] . Alongside this system of reduced rates, the directive in question establishes a "list of exemptions"[34] . The reason for establishing this list of exemptions is the same reason for establishing the possibility of applying reduced rates in certain situations, the protection of certain sectors of activity and the guarantee that certain goods and services are more easily accessible.

2.2 IN PORTUGAL

VAT was introduced in Portugal to replace the so-called "Transaction Tax"[35] . This

---

the autonomous regions of Agores and Madeira and to imports carried out directly in these regions (Article 105, as amended by Council Directive 2009/47/EC of May 5, 2009).

31 Chapter 4 of the directive contains specific provisions whose period of application is limited until the introduction of the definitive system. This definitive system is based on the principle that supplies of goods and services are taxed in the member state of origin (art. 402). A common VAT system, hence the concern to "progressively restrict or abolish derogations (Art. 403 in fine)".

32 Article 110

33 Article 113 enshrines an open clause insofar as it provides for the possibility for member states which, on January 1, 1991, in accordance with Community legislation, granted exemptions with the right to deduct VAT paid in the previous stage, or applied reduced rates below the minimum of 5%, in respect of goods and services not listed in Annex III, to apply the reduced rate or one of the two reduced rates provided for in Article 98 to the supply of such goods or services. Member states which on January 1, 1993 were obliged to increase their standard rate in force on January 1, 1991 by more than 2% may apply a reduced rate of less than the minimum of 5% to the supply of goods and services in the categories listed in Annex III (Article 114). These same member states may apply the same reduced rate to children's clothing, footwear and housing (this possibility was introduced by Council Directive 2009/47/EC of May 5, 2009). As for member states that applied a reduced rate to children's clothing, footwear and housing on January 1, 1991, they can continue to apply this rate to the supply of these goods or services (Article 115). It was also provided that states which at that time applied a reduced rate to the supply of goods and services not listed in Annex III could continue to apply the reduced rate or one of the two reduced rates in Article 98, provided that the rate was not less than 12% (Article 118; this system does not apply to the supply of second-hand goods, works of art, collectors' items or antiques). The reduced rate could also be applied to the supply of live plants and other floricultural products and to the supply of firewood (Article 122). In addition to the situations we've mentioned where reduced rates can be applied, the directive establishes other specific ones for certain member states (Austria (117), Greece (119), the Czech Republic (123), Cyprus (125), Malta (127), Poland (128) and Slovenia (129)).

34 Title IX, Articles 131 to 137. Article 132 establishes "exemptions for the benefit of certain activities of general interest".

35 Approved by Decree-Law No. 47.066, of July 1st, which approved the Transactions Tax Code and entered into force on August 1st, 1966.

was a single-phase tax on wholesalers. As a general consumption tax, it was levied on any goods produced in the country or imported, and from 1979 onwards[36] , it included some services. The Transaction Tax replaced various consumption taxes[37] and was abolished by Decree Law 394-B/84 of December 26, which created the Value Added Tax (VAT). VAT was adopted in our country on January 1, 19 8 6[38] . Despite coinciding with entry into the then European Economic Community (EEC), the adoption of VAT was not imposed as a requirement for entry into the Community. However, as after a transitional period all member states would have to adopt it, Portugal decided to implement it and consequently repeal the Transaction Tax[39] . In fact, in the very preamble of the law that approved the CIVA[40] , at the same time as it refers to EU law on this tax, as a "basic reference point in the construction of the tax system"[41] , that is, in Portugal, it is made clear that the entry into force of the CIVA at a time when "Portugal is not bound by any approximation to the *acquis communautaire* means that the choice of VAT as the general consumption tax model has been disconnected from the effects of joining the EEC to be based on the very merits of VAT in comparison with the single-phase IT system"[4243] .

Outside the context of joining the EEC, there were several reasons given by the Portuguese legislator for adopting VAT as the model for taxing transactions.

---

36 As amended by Decree-Law no. 374-D/79, of September 10th.

37 It has its antecedents in the transfer taxes on movable property and the Value Added Tax on Transactions created by Law No. 1368 of September 21, 1922 and abolished by Decree Law No. 16731 of April 13, 1929.

38 In accordance with Article 10(1) of Decree-Law 394-B/84 of December 26, as amended by Article 1 of Law 42/85 of August 22.

39 Note that when the CIVA was approved (1984) Portugal was a candidate country for membership.

40 VAT was approved by Decree-Law 394-B/84 of December 26, which created the Value Added Tax Code (CIVA).

41 It goes on to say that "various deviations" were "foreseen as necessary, given Portugal's special conditions in relation to most EEC countries", such as: "a set of essential goods - those on list I - is excluded from the objective VAT base, in order to avoid a sudden shift from a narrow-based tax such as IT, covering only around 30% of family expenditure, to a fully broad-based VAT, of the type proposed by the Community directives, the full application of which would lead to around two-thirds of that expenditure being taxed. The exclusion from the tax base is effected by applying the exemption scheme with refund of input taxes, also often referred to as the 'zero-rate scheme', to transactions involving these goods."

42 However, as a candidate country for accession to the EEC, it was decided to consider Community solutions as a necessity when implementing VAT in Portugal, in the name of greater approximation and convergence to the common VAT system imposed by the condition of member state, which would effectively occur on January 1, 1986.

43 By the time VAT was implemented in Portugal, countries such as France, Denmark, Germany, Belgium, Luxembourg and the United Kingdom had already adopted it as a general consumption tax.

Firstly, there were the merits of VAT in the various countries that already had it in place43. On the other hand, the growing financing needs of the public sector, which require an increase in tax revenue. In fact, the Transaction Tax that had been in place up until now revealed some weaknesses that called for its replacement. And this despite successive changes. The levels of tax evasion and fraud in the field of IT grew at an "overwhelming rate", which in addition to subtracting revenue from the state coffers caused "situations of flagrant injustice due to the distortions of competition it caused" 44.

Another of the criticisms levelled at VAT by the legislator when he approved it was the difficulty of combining the taxation of goods at the wholesale level (which characterized VAT) with the extension of the tax's scope to include all services. The extension was necessary for "objectives of fiscal equity and neutrality", but also as a way of increasing the productivity of this general tax, to the detriment of the practicability of excessively high rates, which generate incentives for evasion and fraud and "weaken fiscal morality"45.

It was in this context that VAT was pointed out as involving a much more perfect technique than IT, "ensuring greater neutrality in taxation" and constituting a system with "greater potential for obtaining revenue". Greater neutrality in taxation, insofar as it is levied at all stages of production and is levied on the effective price of the transaction (and not on the *normal value),* the weight of the tax is spread over a greater number of operators[444546] and it becomes more difficult to manipulate taxable values. The "greater potential for raising revenue" can be seen in the possibility allowed by VAT to extend the taxation of transactions to the area of services .[47]

---

44 See the preamble to the law that approved the CIVA.

45 See the preamble of the law that approved the CIVA: "broadening the tax base for consumption taxation is the only way to reconcile the objective of increasing tax revenue with the objective of not practicing unrealistic tax rates that generate discontent among taxpayers and, ultimately, illegitimate evasion".

46 In the case of Transaction Tax, taxpayers were only producers and wholesalers; with VAT, they were also service providers and retailers.

47 We can read in the preamble of the law that approved VAT that "the adoption of VAT will imply a significant broadening of this tax base, an approximation to the broad base that is now the rule in the general taxation of

The introduction of a tax such as VAT into our legal and fiscal system was seen as a fundamental reform. A reform that required effort and willingness to adapt to the different operators involved, both tax authorities and taxable persons, especially those who were not covered by the transaction tax system. In the legislator's view, this was the price of providing the country with a more neutral and productive tax [48].

Despite the fundamental reform, there was a concern not to make an abrupt break with the provisions of the Transaction Tax, even if they did constitute real derogations from the common system of taxation stemming from Community guidelines. Thus, a series of exclusions for the so-called "essential goods" were established in terms of objective taxation. These exclusions are made through what is often referred to as the "zero-rate system", or the system of exemption with reimbursement of input taxes. Opting for this regime has a similar effect to that achieved in the Transaction Tax Code through the complete exemption from tax for the goods listed in List I annexed to it. The point and difference is that the VAT regime sought to shorten the list of goods subject to the special regime, so that it would be reserved for goods whose nature as essential goods (especially foodstuffs) was indisputable[49] . It should be noted, however, that the enshrinement of these benefit schemes was accompanied by a "validity period", since the legislator established their temporary nature from the outset, since they were contrary to Community directives and the full entry into force of the common VAT system would imply the extension of the tax base to those transactions.

On the other hand, an exemption scheme was established for small production

---

consumption in the advanced countries and whose paradigm is the uniform tax base constructed by the 6th Directive[a] . In fact, one of the main advantages of the tax option is that it facilitates the construction of this broad base".

48 "We would only lose out if the desire not to change entrenched habits led us to open up, beyond tolerable limits, exceptions and deviations from the basic rules of how VAT works and its characteristics of generality and neutrality: we would soon see the tax base erode, the main advantages of the tax lost and it transformed into a simulacrum of a general tax, which would ultimately represent no improvement on the previous VAT system."

49 Precisely the same was foreseen for agricultural production goods, restricting to a minimum the list of goods that benefited from the exemption system with upstream reimbursement.

units, i.e. those with a low turnover[50] , which, like final consumers, would bear the tax invoiced by their suppliers.

As far as rates are concerned, a differentiated rate structure was chosen[51] : a reduced rate of 8%, a standard rate of 16% and an increased rate of 30%. The reduced rate was reserved for the set of goods that were part of list I of the Transaction Tax Code, which now no longer benefit from exemption because they are not considered "so essential", but are taxed at a lower rate, and also for some services. The increased rate was established in compliance with the constitutional precept that provides for the taxation of luxury consumption[52] . By excluding parts, anything that wasn't subject to the two aforementioned rates was taxed at the normal rate. This rate structure was chosen with the aim of achieving VAT revenue close to that obtained from the taxes that VAT was intended to replace .[53]

With the establishment of Portugal as a member state and once the transitional period for adapting VAT to Directive 77/388/EEC was over, it became necessary to adapt Portuguese legislation to Community rules. In this context, DL no. 195/89 of June 12 was particularly important[54] . Subsequently, there have been many changes to the CIVA, many of them in compliance with the directives and regulations in force at the time. Given the subject of our study, we will refer to these changes as and when deemed necessary and appropriate.

The title of this dissertation is the implications for fiscal policy, in terms of the treatment and successive changes to VAT, especially in terms of the structure of rates. This is because it seems important to us to address the possibility that fiscal policy, understood as the *"activity of transferring wealth through the creation and*

---

50 Especially prevalent in retail and services.

51 Although we can conclude that the preference, at the limit and on a strictly technical level, would be for a single rate.

52 Article 107(4) of the CRP.

53 Transit tax, railroad tax, tourist tax, see Article 2 of Decree-Law 394-B/84 of December 26.

54 In addition to the objective of adapting the tax to Community standards, this law aimed to adapt it to Personal Income Tax (IRS) and Corporate Income Tax (IRC), since it changed the exemptions for property taxes, professional taxes and industrial contributions. At the same time, it abolished the zero rates for ordinary wines and cinema tickets, while maintaining the zero rate for medicines, books and newspapers (goods which are not included in the Accession Treaty).

collection of taxes"[55] , could be an instrument for carrying out taxation based on assumptions of social and not merely economic-financial concern. Indeed, we cannot forget that the main premise of tax policy is to raise revenue. However, we will analyze whether it can be intended to achieve other goals, such as shaping economic and social behavior .[56]

First, we'll look at fiscal policy.

---

55 NABAIS, CASALTA, Por um Estado Fiscal Suportavel Estudos de Direito Fiscal, volume II, Almedina, 2008, page 42.
56 Instead of being intended to achieve other ends, we will see that it can even become a necessity, given the evolution of human behavior, to remedy or prevent worse evils.

3. FISCAL POLICY

At the heart of fiscal policy are taxes. It has to do, "in micro terms, with what taxes can be created and collected and, in macro terms, with what amount or share of GDP can be demanded in taxes in a market economy, in order to obtain the means of financing necessary to achieve the objectives that the public authorities have set"[57] . This means that fiscal policy[58] will encompass those decisions made in the field of taxes, with a view to fulfilling the objectives set by the rulers of a given country.

Fiscal policy is linked to budgetary policy. Budgetary policy is the process of determining the necessary public expenditure and how to support it. It defines the amount to be spent and how it is to be paid for (what revenue is to be raised and by what means). Given that the main source of funding for our state, and for most countries, is taxes, we can easily see the link between fiscal policy and government policy. In fact, fiscal policy cannot fail to be taken into account when, as part of budgetary policy, a certain amount of public expenditure is to be covered by taxes. This relationship is present at both the economic and social levels. At the economic level, insofar as decision-makers must foresee the consequences for economic development and activity of choosing different taxes to cover expenditure; at the social level, since those same decision-makers, justifying that it is in the general interest, can choose to benefit certain social groups. This can be done through fiscal policy, by means of tax breaks, or through budgetary policy, by instituting direct subsidies.

Defining a fiscal policy is particularly important in a state like ours, a fiscal state. It is fiscal because it relies fundamentally on taxes for its financial support. In fact, there are reasons why our state should be considered a fiscal state. On the one hand, there are a number of state tasks that are public in nature, in the sense that they aim

---

57 NABAIS, CASALTA, op. cit., page 43.
58 Or fiscal policies, as Dr. Casalta Nabais refers to in his book, referring to the whole group of fiscal policies adopted in the various sectors of public activity.

to meet collective needs, and, on the other hand, there are tasks that, although they aim to satisfy individual needs, cannot fail to be financed by taxes, in compliance with constitutional obligations (such as free compulsory education, health and justice, free for those who suffer from economic insufficiency). And this characteristic, that of a fiscal state, is a prerequisite for the existence of a fiscal policy.[59]

Looking at the Portuguese context, we can see, following closely Law No. 66-A/2012, of December 31[60], which approved the Major Planning Options for 2013, that for that year, tax policy will have the following strategic lines: a) continuing the structural reform of the tax administration; b) strengthening the fight against and evasion of tax and customs fraud; c) broadening the tax base and restructuring rates; d) broadening the network of agreements to avoid double taxation signed with other states. Concerns about greater simplification, control and, consequently, revenue are emerging."[61] . Broadening the tax base and restructuring the rates of the various taxes is justified as possibly resulting in legal simplification and an equitable distribution of the additional effort of budgetary consolidation by means of taxation, a tax which is assumed in the Economic and Financial Adjustment Program.[62]

In terms of international tax policy, the aim is to extend the network of conventions to avoid double taxation and also to combat tax fraud and evasion.

Specifically in terms of VAT, there have been no changes in tax rates, but the exemption for the agricultural sector has been revoked and it is now taxed, albeit at

---

59 NABAIS, CASALTA, op. cit., page 45.

60 Law no. 66-A/2012, of December 31, page 14 point 2.4.

61 "In order for the tax system to be fairer and more equitable, it is crucial, on the one hand, to promote a broadening of the tax base and for everyone to be called upon to contribute according to their real ability to pay and, on the other, for the tax administration to have the operational capacity to control and monitor situations of tax evasion." NABAIS, CASALTA, op. cit., page 15.

62 Portugal officially requested financial assistance from the European Union, the eurozone member states and the International Monetary Fund (IMF) on April 7, 2011. This assistance is intended to support a program of policies to restore confidence and allow the economy to return to sustainable growth, while preserving financial stability in Portugal, the eurozone and the EU. The loan agreement was approved by the European Council and signed on May 17, 2011. The IMF's Executive Board approved the agreement under its Extended Fund Facility on May 20, 2011, available at: http://ec.europa.eu/portugal/temas/ajuda_economica_portugal/index_pt.htm

a reduced rate .[63]

This line of thinking is, in a way, carried over from previous years. In fact, in Law 64-A/2011 of December 30, 2011, which approved the Major Planning Options for 2012-2015, the need to justify the budgetary options with the need to comply with the commitments made by the Portuguese state in the EFAP (Economic and Financial Aid Program) is clearly stated .[64]

In terms of Value Added Tax, there have been major changes. Exemptions have been reduced and the tax lists annexed to the CIVA have been restructured and rationalized, as we will discuss in this study[65] , with the transfer of categories of goods and services between the different lists and the repeal of some of them, thus moving to the standard tax rate, *"thus avoiding a rise in the current tax rates"".* However, the law states that *"the application of the reduced rate to the basket of essential goods and services, namely basic food products, medicines, pharmaceutical products and transport (...) has* been preserved *as a way of protecting the most vulnerable social groups from the impact of budgetary consolidation measures. At the same time, the scope of goods subject to the intermediate rate has been considerably reduced, while ensuring that it is maintained for a limited number of goods that are crucial to national production sectors, such as wine-growing, agriculture and fisheries.""* As a way of strengthening social policies, it is determined that *"part of the additional VAT revenue generated by this restructuring will be allocated to financing the Social Emergency Program, increasing the resources allocated to helping Portuguese families affected by exclusion and social deprivation".*

Having done this analysis, and particularly in terms of VAT, we can ask the question that gave rise to this study: what are the implications for tax policy?

---

63 Chapter 4, point 4.2.

64 "which includes a wide range of fiscal measures, essential for pursuing the imperative goal of reducing the general government deficit to 7645 million euros (4.5% of GDP) in 2012. This effort is crucial to regaining credibility at home and abroad, in a macroeconomic context marked by reduced domestic demand and a high degree of uncertainty regarding the international environment."

65 Chapter 4.

Before any attempt at an answer, let's not forget, as we mentioned earlier, that the main objective pursued by tax policy is to raise revenue. However, **can it pursue other objectives, such as shaping economic and social behavior?** In the latter case, and whenever we have taxes for that purpose, they are commonly referred to as *non-tax taxes*. This is because true (fiscal) taxes are aimed almost exclusively at collecting revenue for the state coffers; *extra-fiscal* taxes, on the other hand, put the purpose of raising revenue on the back burner and reveal other intentions[66] . They can be levied to ensure a fair distribution of income and wealth[67] , to finance certain public services, or even to prevent certain behaviors .[68]

The context in which we pose the question is somewhat challenging.

In fact, the current global economic crisis has required governments to make an extra effort, as they are forced to find strategies to stimulate their economies in order to get out of recession and achieve some stability. This desire for stability is important because it can help prevent recurrences. In the medium and long term, governments will have to pay the costs of the crisis, balance their budgets and promote growth and development[69] . In this context, there is talk of the need to change the target of revenue raising, moving from taxing income (of natural and legal persons) and social security contributions to taxing consumption and property. Within consumption taxation, it is claimed that VAT would be more efficient if the base for applying the standard rate were broadened, with the inherent removal of most exemptions, zero rates and reduced rates. The introduction of a broader tax base, as well as the generalized application of the standard rate, would generate more revenue at less cost, as we will discuss later in this study. Now, if there is a need to modernize the VAT system[70] , in order to adapt it to new and current

---

66 Of an economic and social nature.

67 See Article 103(1) of the Constitution of the Portuguese Republic.

68 One example is Spain's autonomous taxes on uncultivated land.

69 PALMA, CLOTILDE CELORICO, "The Commission's recent communication on the future of VAT", TOC magazine no. 144, March 2012, available at: http://www.otoc.pt/fotos/editor2/gabineestudos144.pdf, "the financial crisis has exposed member states to a double challenge in terms of economic policy: encouraging sustainable economic growth and consolidating public finances".

70 It should be noted that since the adoption of the Green Paper on the future of VAT (2010), the Commission has

demands, why not take this opportunity to question the purposes of the tax: are they merely economic? Or will it have a markedly social and extra-fiscal aspect?

In the excerpts above from the laws approving the major ornamental budgets for the current and previous year, it seems to us that, only in a very subtle way, some social concern can be seen in the changes made to VAT. There is an express reference to the need for simplification, for broadening the tax base, for combating tax evasion and fraud, but with a view, it seems to us, to collecting revenue more effectively. The social aspect will lie in maintaining privileged treatment for a range of goods and services, with the most disadvantaged and vulnerable in mind. As we've already said, it's challenging...

---

received more than
one thousand seven hundred contributions (from businesses, academics, citizens and tax authorities), in response to the call for critical reflection on all aspects of the VAT system in the EU. These contributions, as well as a report on them, are available at:
http://ec.europa.eu/taxation_customs/common/consultations/tax/2010_11_future_vat_en.htm

4. FEES

Taxable transactions are subject to VAT at the rates and conditions maintained by each state in which they take place. The rates are set as a percentage of the taxable value of the transfer of goods and services subject to tax, which is generally the value of the consideration obtained or to be obtained from the purchaser, the recipient or a third party .[72]

In our case, the VAT rates are laid down in Article 18 of the CIVA, which we will now analyze.

4.1 ANALYSIS OF ARTICLE 18 OF CIVA

In terms of tax rates, the Portuguese legislator is limited by Community guidance[73] . In fact, the VAT Directive[74] states that member states can have two reduced tax rates, between 5% and 12%, and a standard rate of between 15% and 25%. The same directive also establishes under what conditions member states can apply the reduced rates, limiting this application to the goods and services listed in its Annex III .[75]

Our CIVA establishes, in its Article 18[76] , the VAT rates to be applied on the mainland and in the autonomous regions, since they are different[77] . The **reduced**

---

72 See Article 16(1) of the CIVA.

73 The current VAT rate structure was adopted by the Council in 1992 as part of a package of measures deemed necessary for the abolition of border controls and the creation of the Internal Market. VAT is a Community tax, which "presupposes its application in the Member States, under conditions of competition and in line with the fundamental principles or freedoms of the EU", TEIXEIRA, GLORIA, Manual de Direito Fiscal, 2ª edigao, Almedina, 2010, pag. 198.

74 Directive 2006/112/EC, Articles 96 to 99.

75 This Annex III was reformulated by Directive 2009/47 of May 5, published in OJ No. L116 of May 9, 2009. This directive also made a specific change for Portugal to Article 105 of the VAT Directive, which now states that "Portugal may apply one of the two reduced rates provided for in Article 98 to tolls on bridges in the Lisbon area." On this subject, see what has already been said in this work, chapter 2, point 2.1.

76 The fees in article 18 are the result of the wording given to this article by Law 55-A/2010, of December 31.

77 The possibility of Portugal applying lower rates in the autonomous regions was expressly enshrined in the Sixth Directive with definitive force in Article 12(6), which now corresponds to Article 105 of the VAT Directive. For the mainland (Article 18(1)) we have the reduced rate of 6%, the intermediate rate of 13% and the standard rate of 23%. For the autonomous regions (Article 18(3)), the reduced rate is 4% (Agores) and 5% (Madeira), the intermediate rate is 9% (Agores) and 12% (Madeira) and, finally, the standard rate is 16% (Agores) and 22% (Madeira).

77 The goods and services included in this list I are as follows:

- Food products (item 1): such as cereals and preparations made from cereals, meat and edible meat offal, fresh or

---

frozen, of bovine animals, swine, sheep, goats, horses, poultry and rabbits, fish and molluscs, milk and dairy products, birds' eggs, fats and oils, fresh fruit, vegetables and horticultural products, water, bee honey, salt (sodium chloride), fruit or horticultural juices and nectars and dietetic products intended for enteric nutrition and gluten-free products for celiac patients (items 1. 1 to 1.12).1 a 1.12).
- Other (budget 2), such as:
- Newspapers, general information magazines and other periodicals dealing predominantly with material of a scientific, educational, literary, artistic, cultural, recreational or sporting nature and books on all physical media. (item 2.1) - With the exception of publications or books of an obscene or pornographic nature, considered as such in the relevant legislation, and works bound in leather, silk or similar fabrics. - Audiovisual levy collected to finance the public broadcasting service. (item 2.2) - Newsprint, referred to in subheading 48.01 of the harmonized system. (item 2.3) - This item includes napkins and diapers. - Pharmaceutical and similar products and their active substances listed below (item 2.5): a) Medicines, pharmaceutical specialties and other pharmaceutical products intended exclusively for therapeutic and prophylactic purposes; b) Condoms; c) Pastes, gauze, hydrophilic cotton, adhesive strips and dressings and other similar supports, whether or not impregnated or coated with any substance, for hygienic, medicinal or surgical uses; d) Medicinal plants, roots and tubers in their natural state; e) Blood glucose, glucosuria and acetonuria strips, needles, syringes and pens for administering insulin used in the prevention and treatment of diabetes mellitus. - Orthopaedic appliances, medical-surgical belts and stockings, wheelchairs and similar hand- or motor-operated vehicles for the disabled, appliances, devices and other prosthetic or compensatory equipment intended to replace, in whole or in part, any limb or organ of the human body or for the treatment of fractures and lenses for correcting sight, as well as orthopaedic footwear, provided it is prescribed by a doctor. (item 2.6)
- Bras, swimsuits or other garment handles for medical use, consisting of inner pockets, intended for the placement of prostheses used by mastectomized women. (item 2.8) - Utensils and any appliances or objects specifically designed for use by people with disabilities, provided that they appear on a list approved by joint order of the Ministers of Finance, Solidarity and Social Security and Health. (item 2.9) - Utensils and any other equipment exclusively or mainly intended for rescue and salvage operations purchased by humanitarian associations and fire brigades, as well as by the Instituto Socorros Naufil (Rescue Institute).9) - Utensils and other equipment exclusively or mainly intended for rescue and salvage operations acquired by humanitarian associations and fire departments, as well as by the Shipwreck Relief Institute and SANAS - Voluntary Nautical Salvage Corps. (item 2.10) - Chairs and seats suitable for transporting children in motor vehicles, as well as other restraint equipment for the same purpose (item 2.29).
- Agricultural production goods (item 3), such as: - Fertilizers, fertilizers and soil improvers. (item 3.1) - Live animals intended solely or principally for agricultural work, slaughter or breeding. (item 3.2) - Flour, residues and waste from the food industry and any other products suitable for feeding livestock and other animals, including farmed fish, intended for human consumption. (item 3.3) - Plant protection products. (item 3.4) - Seeds, bulbs and propagules. (item 3.5) - Fodder and straw. (item 3.6) - Live plants of forest or fruit species. (item 3.7) - Olive pomace and other oil seeds, grape pips and husks (item 3.8) - Cupric sulphate, ferric sulphate and double sulphate of copper and iron (item 3.9) - Sublimed sulphur (item 3.10)
- Transfers of goods made in the context of the following agricultural production activities (item 5)- (This item was added to list I annexed to the CIVA by the State Budget Law for 2013, Law No. 66-B/2012, of December 31): - Culture as such: (item 5.1) - Agriculture in general, including viticulture; (item 5.1.1) - Fruit-growing (including oil-growing) and floral and ornamental horticulture, including in greenhouses; (item 5.1.2) - Production of mushrooms, spices, seeds and vegetative propagating material; nurseries. Agricultural activities that are not related to land use or where land use is merely an accessory, such as hydroponic crops and production in pots, trays and other self-supporting means, are excluded. (item 5.1.3) - Animal husbandry related to land use or in which land use is essential: (item 5.2) - Animal husbandry; (item 5.2.1) - Poultry farming; (item 5.2.2) - Rabbit farming; (item 5.2.3) - Sericulture; (item 5.2.4) - Heliciculture; (item 5.2.5) - Aquaculture and fish farming; (item 5.2.6) - Caniculture; (item 5.2.7) - Breeding of song, ornamental and fantasy birds; (item 5.2.8) - Breeding of animals for fur or laboratory experiments; (item 5.2.9) - Beekeeping; (item 5.3) - Forestry; (item 5.4) - The processing activities carried out by an agricultural producer on products derived essentially from his agricultural production with the means normally used on agricultural and forestry holdings are also considered to be agricultural production activities. (item 5.5)
78 As for services taxed at a reduced rate, we have:
- The supply of medical and health services and closely related operations carried out by hospitals, clinics, dispensaries and similar establishments not belonging to legal persons governed by public law or to private institutions integrated into the National Health Service, when they waive the exemption, under the terms of Article 12(1)(b) of the VAT Code. (item no. 2.7)
Services rendered in the exercise of the legal profession to unemployed persons and workers in the context of legal proceedings of a labor nature and to persons benefiting from legal aid. (item 2.11) - Passenger transport, including rental

rate of 6% applies to imports, transfers of goods and services listed in **List I annexed to the CIVA** (Article 18(1)(a)) .[77][78]

- The **intermediate rate of** 13%, on the other hand, applies to imports, transfers of goods and services listed in **List II annexed to the CIVA**[78][79] (Article 18(1)(b)) .[80]

---

of vehicles with driver. (item 2.14) - This item includes the transport service and the price supplement required for luggage and seat reservations. - Accommodation in hotel-type establishments. (item 2.17) - Building work for affordable housing or controlled-cost housing, regardless of the developer, provided that this classification is certified by the competent authority of the relevant ministry. (item 2.18) - Contracts for immovable property in which local authorities, municipal companies whose purpose is urban rehabilitation and management wholly owned by public bodies, associations of municipalities, public companies responsible for the public network of secondary schools or associations and fire departments are the owners of the work, provided that, in any case, said works are contracted directly with the contractor. (item 2.19) - Rental of reserved areas in camping and caravanning sites, including services closely linked to them. (item 2.20) - Tolls on road crossings over the Tagus, in Lisbon. (item 2.21) - Provision of services related to the cleaning of public roads, as well as the collection, storage, transportation, recovery and disposal of waste. (item 2.22) - Urban rehabilitation contracts, as defined by specific legislation, carried out on buildings or public spaces located in urban rehabilitation areas (critical areas for urban recovery and reconversion, intervention areas for urban rehabilitation societies and others) delimited under the terms of the law, or within the scope of requalification and rehabilitation operations of recognized national public interest. (item 2.23) - Building rehabilitation contracts which, regardless of location, are contracted directly by the Institute for Housing and Urban Rehabilitation (IHRU), as well as those carried out under special financial or tax support schemes for building rehabilitation or under programs financially supported by the IHRU. (item 2.24) - Real estate construction contracts and related service contracts whose promoters are housing and construction cooperatives, including those carried out by housing and economic construction cooperative unions for their member cooperatives within the scope of their statutory activities, provided that the dwellings fall within the scope of the social housing policy, namely when they comply with the concept and parameters of cost-controlled housing, increased by 20%, provided that they are certified by the National Housing Institute. (item 2.25) - Contracts for the maintenance, repair and improvement of buildings or part of urban housing buildings owned by housing and construction cooperatives transferred to their members under a collective ownership regime, whatever the respective modality. (item 2.26) - Contracts for the improvement, remodeling, renovation, restoration, repair or maintenance of real estate or autonomous parts thereof used for residential purposes, with the exception of cleaning work, maintenance of green spaces and contracts for real estate covering all or part of the constituent elements of swimming pools, saunas, tennis courts, golf or mini-golf courses or similar facilities. (item 2.27) - The reduced rate does not cover the materials incorporated, unless their value does not exceed 20% of the total value of the services provided. - The provision of home care services for children, the elderly, drug addicts, the sick or disabled (item 2.28) - The provision of maintenance or repair services for prostheses, equipment, apparatus, artifacts and other goods referred to in items 2.6, 2.8 and 2.9 (item 2.30) - The provision of forestry services (item 4):
services of cleaning and cultural intervention in stands, carried out on agricultural and forestry holdings. - Services that contribute to agricultural production, namely the following (item 4.2): (This item was added to list I annexed to the CIVA by the State Budget Law for 2013, Law No. 66-B/2012, of December 31.) a) Sowing, planting, harvesting, threshing, baling, reaping, collecting and transporting; b) Packaging and wrapping, such as drying, cleaning, crushing, disinfecting and ensiling agricultural products; c) Storing agricultural products; d) Keeping, rearing and fattening animals; f) Technical assistance; g) The destruction of harmful plants and animals and the treatment of plants and land by spraying; h) The operation of irrigation and drainage facilities; i) Tree pruning, wood cutting and other forestry operations.
79 This list underwent significant changes with Law 64-B/2011 of December 30, which approved the State Budget for 2012; see Article 123(2) of that law, which revoked fifteen appropriations.
80 Products for human consumption (item 1), such as: Preserved meat and edible meat offal (item 1.1) - (Only preserved meat and edible meat offal that has not undergone any processing or been included in a preparation, beyond the mere preservation process); Preserved fish and molluscs (item 1.2), with the exception of oysters; ordinary wines (item 1.10); spring, mineral, medicinal and table waters, aerated waters and waters containing added carbon dioxide, with the exception of waters containing added substances (item 1.11); other, such as (item 2): Oil and gas oil, colored and marked, and fuel oil and mixtures thereof (item 2.3); Agricultural implements and equipment, mobile silos, power tillers, motor

All imports, transfers of goods and services not covered by the reduced and intermediate rates are taxed at the **standard rate of** 23% (Article 18(1)(c) of the CIVA).

It should be noted that the rate applicable to the tax transaction is that in force at the time the tax becomes payable .[81]

On the other hand, it is worth mentioning the legal resolution for situations involving the transfer of goods that have as their object several goods that make up a different commercial product. Whenever the goods that make up the unit of sale do not change their nature or lose their individuality, the rate applicable to the overall value of the goods is that which corresponds to them or, if different rates apply, the highest; whenever the goods that make up the unit of sale change their nature and quality or lose their individuality, the rate applicable to the whole (as a new product and different from its constituent elements) is that which, as such, corresponds to them .[82]

4.2 HISTORICAL OVERVIEW OF CHANGES IN VAT RATES

As we explained earlier, VAT was introduced into our legal system and tax system in 1986. Since then, there have been constant changes to the rates. Initially, three rates were set: a reduced rate of 8%, a standard rate of 16% and an increased rate (for luxury consumption) of 30%[83] . In 1992, the reduced rate for the mainland was lowered to 5%, which was maintained until June 30, 2010, as from July 1 of this year the reduced rate was raised to 6%. The standard rate fluctuated between 16% and 17% between 1986 and 2001. From June 5, 2002, it went up to 19%, and rose

---

pumps, electric pumps, agricultural tractors, classified as such in the respective booklets, and other machinery and apparatus used solely or principally in agriculture, livestock farming or forestry. (item 2.5); Entry to singing, dancing, music, theater, cinema, bullfighting and circus shows (item 2.6) - except for entry to shows of a pornographic or obscene nature, as considered in the relevant legislation.

81 Article 18(9) of the CIVA.

82 Article 18(4) of the CIVA.

83 This is for the mainland. For the autonomous regions, the rates were set at 6%, 12% and 21% (reduced, normal and increased, respectively).

again to 21% in 2005. In 2008 and 2009 there was a 20% drop[84] . Law no. 12-A/2010 of June 30 amended the wording of paragraphs a) to c) of no. 1 and no. 3 of article 18 of the VAT Code, an amendment that came into force on July 1, 2010. In effect, the reduced VAT rate is now 6% for transactions carried out on the mainland, and remains at 4% for transactions that are considered[85] to have been carried out in the Autonomous Regions. The intermediate rate has risen to 13% and 9%, depending on whether the operations are carried out on the Mainland or in the Autonomous Regions respectively, and finally, the standard rate has risen to 21% and 15%.

Also in 2010, in the State Budget Law for 2011[86] , there was another change in this area. That law amended the wording of Article 18(1)(c) and (3) and Article 49, both of the VAT Code (CIVA), as well as Article 1(1) of Decree-Law 347/85 of August 23. These changes came into force on the mainland and in the autonomous regions on 01.01.2011. According to these changes, the standard rate of VAT became, from the date mentioned above, 23% for operations carried out on the mainland and 16% for operations considered to be carried out in the autonomous regions. This law introduced changes to the lists annexed to the VAT code[87] , which list the goods subject to lower rates. Focusing on these changes, since they are closely related to the subject we are discussing, let's look at the changes to list I, which lists the goods subject to the reduced rate. In item 2.1[88] , the scope of application has been broadened to include scientific, literary and artistic materials, in addition to those of a cultural, educational, recreational and sporting nature. At the same time, it now includes general information magazines and other periodicals, as long as they deal with the materials mentioned therein, and no longer applies only to magazines or

---

84 Law 26-A/2008 of June 27 changed the standard rate from 21% to 20%.

85 In accordance with Article 1(2) and (3) of Decree-Law 347/85 of August 23rd.

86 Law No. 55-A/2010, of December 31.

87 Article 103 of Law 55-A/2010 of December 31.

88 "Newspapers, general information magazines and other periodicals dealing predominantly with material of a scientific, educational, literary, artistic, cultural, recreational or sporting nature, and books on all physical media.
With the exception of publications or books of an obscene or pornographic nature, considered as such in the relevant legislation, and works bound in leather, silk or similar fabrics".

periodicals with a specific theme. Also included in this budget are books, on all physical media[89] . The availability of books electronically is excluded. In accordance with Article 18(7) of the CIVA, the provision of services electronically is subject to the standard rate.

Item 2.11[90] of the same list will also undergo changes, especially with regard to its scope. The universe of recipients of the reduced rate for services rendered in the exercise of the professions of lawyer, attorney and solicitor has become more restricted, insofar as services rendered by these professionals to pensioners, unemployed people in legal proceedings that are not of an employment nature, and to any interested party in proceedings on the status of persons, will no longer be taxed at the reduced rate .[91]

Lastly, item 2.15[92] was amended in 2007 by Law 67-A/2007 of December 31, which led it to include sporting events and the practice of physical and sporting activities. With the amendment under analysis, the exceptions provided for in points a) and b) are maintained, but the practice of physical and sporting activities is now taxed at the normal rate.

Article 104 of Law 55-A/2010 determined the repeal of item 2.4 of list I. In view of the new wording of item 2.1 and the repeal of item 2.4, brochures and other non-periodical publications of a cultural, educational, recreational and sporting nature, whether in paperback or bound, no longer benefit from the reduced rate and are now taxed at the standard rate. The same article also repeals item 2.13 of the same list, which included tools and other equipment exclusively or mainly intended for firefighting and fire detection, which will now also be taxed at the standard rate, without prejudice to the application of the reduced rate to the tools and equipment

---

89 For example, in CD or DVD format.

90 "Services rendered in the exercise of the legal profession to unemployed people and workers in the context of legal proceedings of a labor nature and to people benefiting from legal aid."

91 The exclusion of these categories does not prevent them from benefiting from the reduced VAT rate in cases in which they receive legal aid.

92 which was replaced by the following: "Shows, competitions and sporting events and other public entertainment. Exceptions: a) ... b) ... "

provided for in item 2.10[93] of the same list, when purchased by the entities mentioned therein.

Lastly, article 105 of the same law repeals items 2.1 and 2.2[94] of list II annexed to the CIVA.

Under the State Budget Law for 2012, Law 64-B/2011 of December 30, which came into force on January 1, 2012, there were new changes to the lists annexed to the CIVA.

The wording of sections 1.4.9, 1.7 and 1.11 of list I has been amended. From section 1.4.9[95] , soy desserts have been removed and are now subject to the standard rate. As for item 1.7[95] [96] , this amendment makes only drinking water provided by drinking water networks subject to the reduced rate. Spring water, mineral water, medicinal water, table water, carbonated water and water containing carbon dioxide are now subject to the intermediate rate. Waters containing other substances remain subject to the normal rate. Lastly, item 1.11[97] no longer covers soft drinks, as well as syrups, concentrated drinks and concentrated juice products, which will now be taxed at the standard rate.

Sections 14.8 and 1.10[98] have been repealed and will now be subject to the standard rate.

Heading *2.15,* which we mentioned when we explained the changes resulting from the 2011 LOE, has changed again. This time the item was repealed, with the result that tickets to singing, dancing, music, theater, cinema, bullfighting and circus performances, with the exception of those of a pornographic or obscene nature, would now be subject to the intermediate rate of 13%, by adding item 2.6 to list II.

---

93 "Utensils and other equipment exclusively or mainly intended for rescue and salvage operations acquired by humanitarian associations and fire departments, as well as by the Shipwreck Relief Institute and SANAS - Voluntary Nautical Salvage Corps." (item 2.10).

94 They included cut flowers, foliage for ornamentation and decorative floral compositions and ornamental plants.

95 "Soy drinks and yogurts, including tofu."

96 "Water, with the exception of spring, mineral, medicinal and table water, aerated water or water containing added carbon dioxide or other substances."

97 "Fruit or vegetable juices and nectars."

98 1.4.8 - dairy drinks and desserts and 1.10 - peeled fresh potatoes, whole or cut, pre-fried, chilled, frozen, dried or dehydrated, whether or not pureed or prepared by boiling or frying

Tickets to other shows, sporting events and other public entertainment are now subject to the standard rate .[99]

With regard to list II (goods and services subject to the intermediate rate), under item 2.3[100] , heating oil has been removed and is now subject to the standard rate of tax. Items 1.11 on water[101] and 2.6 on tickets to shows[102] , which we mentioned earlier, have been added.

Lastly, a wide range of funds were repealed, with goods and services subject to the standard rate .[103]

Under the 2013 State Budget Law, Law 66-B/2012, of December 31, which came into force on January 1, 2013, repealed Article 9(33), as well as Annexes A and B of the CIVA, with effect from April 1, 2013. Therefore, as of that date, the transfer of goods in the context of agricultural production and the provision of agricultural services are no longer exempt from VAT, but are subject to taxation, albeit with the right to deduct the tax paid on purchases made by the respective taxable persons[104] . In order to mitigate the effects of the repeal of the exemption, that law, taking advantage of the option provided for in paragraph 11) of Annex III of the VAT Directive[105] , introduced new changes to List I annexed to the CIVA, relating to the

---

99 Natural raffia was also taxed at the standard rate, due to the repeal of section 3.11.

100 "Oil and gas oil, colored and marked, and fuel oil and mixtures thereof"

101 Spring, mineral, medicinal and table waters, aerated waters or waters containing carbon dioxide, with the exception of waters containing other substances.

102 Tickets to singing, dancing, music, theater, cinema, bullfighting and circus performances. Tickets to shows of a pornographic or obscene nature, considered as such in the relevant legislation, are excluded.

103 1.3- Fruit and nuts: 1.3.1- Preserved fruit or nuts, namely in sauces, brine or syrup, their jams, jellies, marmalades or pastes; 1.3.2- Fruit and nuts, with or without peel.

1.4- Horticultural products: 1.4.1- Canned horticultural products, particularly in sauces, vinegar or brine, and jams. 1.5- Edible fats and oils: 1.5.1- Directly edible oils and mixtures thereof (edible oils); 1.5.2- Margarines of animal and vegetable origin. 1.6- Green or raw coffee, roasted, ground or ground, its substitutes and mixtures. 1.7- Snacks made from vegetables and seeds. 1.8- Prepared products based on meat, fish, vegetables or horticultural products, stuffed pasta, pizzas, sandwiches and soups, even if presented in a frozen or pre-frozen state and ready-to-eat meals, under the ready-to-eat and take-away or home delivery schemes. 1.9- Snacks based on wheat corn starch, ground and fried corn or potato starch, in individual packages. 2.4- Apparatus, machinery and other equipment intended solely or principally for: a) Capturing and using solar, wind and geothermal energy; b) Capturing and using other alternative forms of energy; c) Energy products from the incineration or transformation of waste, garbage and other residues; d) Prospecting and researching for oil and/or developing the discovery of oil and natural gas; e) Measuring and monitoring to prevent or reduce various forms of pollution. 3- Provision of services: 3.1- Provision of food and beverage services.

104 The purpose of these changes is primarily due to the need felt by the tax authorities to control the agricultural sector.

105 Annex III contains the list of supplies of goods and services to which the reduced rates provided for in Article 98 may apply. Point 11) refers to the supply of goods and services of a kind normally used in agricultural production,

application of the reduced rate, including the goods and services provided for in Article 9(33) of the CIVA .[106]

excluding capital goods such as machinery or buildings;

106 4.2- Provision of services that contribute to the realization of agricultural production, namely the following: a) Sowing, planting, harvesting, threshing, baling, reaping, collecting and transporting; b) Packaging and wrapping, such as drying, cleaning, crushing, disinfecting and ensiling agricultural products; c) The storage of agricultural products; d) The keeping, breeding and fattening of animals; e) The leasing, for agricultural purposes, of the means normally used on agricultural and forestry holdings; f) Technical assistance; g) The destruction of harmful plants and animals and the treatment of

5. EXEMPTIONS, ZERO VAT, REDUCED RATES

Transactions on goods and services are either taxed or exempt. However, the exemptions in the VAT system generally do not completely relieve the transaction of tax, because the suppliers exempt from VAT on their sales are taxed on their purchases.

Zero-rating VAT means that the supplier is fully compensated for the VAT he pays on the products he purchases (inputs). It differs from the exempt trader/supplier in that he pays VAT on his purchases and acquisitions, but is not entitled to use the amount he has paid as a credit that he can impose on his (exempt) sales. This supplier is treated as a final consumer[707] . The *zero-rated* supplier, on the other hand, recovers all the tax on its inputs and has no tax on its outputs, so anyone who buys from this supplier buys the goods or services tax-free.

The concern of the VAT Directive (second directive), expressed in its preamble, is that exemptions can cause difficulties and, moreover, some inequities. That's why the number and scope of exemptions should be reduced as much as possible. Therefore, the current list of exemptions approved by the EU is extremely limited [107108]

If a state, either for social or economic reasons, wants to implement a reduced rate, it shouldn't do so through a rate so low that it doesn't absorb the deductions due for the tax paid in the previous steps. *In theory, zero rating should be used when the*

---

h) The operation of irrigation and drainage facilities; i) Tree pruning, wood cutting and other forestry operations. 5- Transfers of goods carried out in the context of the following agricultural production activities: 5.1- Crop cultivation: 5.1.1- Agriculture in general, including viticulture; 5.1.2- Fruit growing (including olive growing) and floral and ornamental horticulture, including in greenhouses; 5.1.3- Production of mushrooms, spices, seeds and vegetative propagation material; nursery operations. Agricultural activities that are not related to land use or where land use is merely an accessory, namely hydroponic crops and production in pots, trays and other autonomous means of support, are excluded. 5.2- Animal husbandry related to land use or where it is essential: 5.2.1- Animal husbandry; 5.2.2- Poultry farming; 5.2.3- Rabbit farming; 5.2.4- Sericulture; 5.2.5- Heliciculture; 5.2.6- Aquaculture and fish farming; 5.2.7- Caniculture; 5.2.8- Breeding of song, ornamental and fantasy birds; 5.2.9- Raising animals for fur or laboratory experiments; 5.3- Beekeeping; 5.4- Forestry; 5.5- Processing activities carried out by an agricultural producer on products derived essentially from his agricultural production with the means normally used on agricultural and forestry holdings are also considered agricultural production activities.

107 "Is out of the VAT system" TAIT, ALAN, Value Added Tax: International Practice and Problems, International Monetary Fund, 1988, page 49

108 Basically exports, postal services, education, cultural services and financial services.

authorities really wish to ensure that a product is to be free of VAT[109][110][111] . Using a VAT exemption means that the tax is borne by the trader, and if that trader sells to the public, he has to pass on the tax he has borne on inputs to the public by including it in his price or reducing payments to his factors of production (capital and labor). This might suggest that countries that really want to pass on the VAT benefits of free goods and services to the consumer should be allowed to use zero-rating instead of exemptions. However, it turned out that, in practice, countries "frowned" on the use of zero-rating and preferred exemptions.

In Alan Tait's words, zero-rating is used to a very limited extent, even though it is the only real way of guaranteeing a free supply of value added tax[110][111] . At EU level, zero-rating is not a mechanism that should be given priority in use. In fact, Article 28(2) of the Sixth Directive lays down the temporality of the measure, stating that "they may be maintained until a date to be fixed by the Council". The Commission's tendency has therefore been to gradually implement the abolition of zero rates.

As far as reduced rates are concerned, some positive effects are noted and, under their pretext, Member States widely apply different VAT rates, creating a highly diversified and extremely complex VAT system[112] . The main objectives evoked for the application of lower rates are: 1) the promotion of employment, driven by the reduction of wages and the increase in demand;

2) to increase productivity; 3) to promote certain goods/products in order to boost cultural awareness or the health of the population, and 4) to support disadvantaged groups.

With regard to the first, it is argued that a prolonged reduction in the tax rate will be reflected in a reduction in the price of the good or service in question. This

---

109 Idem, page 51

110 Idem, page 53

111 The first country to use zero-rating was the Netherlands, for exports. Instead of exempting as the Directive required, that country taxed exports at a zero rate, which allowed the supplier/exporter to claim the entire tax paid on inputs as a credit.

112 COPENHAGEN ECONOMICS, Study on reduced VAT applied to goods and services in the Member States of the European Union, Final report, dated 21.06.2007, page 8.

reduction in price will increase the demand for such goods or services as they are more accessible. If demand is higher, it will be necessary to increase production to meet that new demand. This increase in production will ultimately promote employment.

Provided they are applied in selected sectors, reduced rates can provide some advantages, even in terms of employment, when the locally supplied services sector employs many low-skilled workers. The argument is that reduced VAT rates, by boosting demand for such services, stimulate demand for low-skilled workers and consequently promote an increase in their wages, so that employment becomes a more attractive option than unemployment.

The issue of productivity is associated with areas that don't usually generate tax revenue, because they include work that is carried out by taxpayers themselves *(do-it-yourself work),* such as housework and small repairs. Taxing such work may encourage taxpayers to do the work themselves, rather than buying it, which could lead to skilled workers devoting their time to domestic work, for example, which is less demanding in terms of skills, rather than to their jobs, where they are more productive. Subjecting such sectors to reduced VAT rates could induce people to spend fewer hours on *do-it-yourself work* and apply themselves more to their work, thus increasing productivity and labor supply. In turn, this could contribute to the transition of elements of the shadow economy into the formal economy sector.[113]

In conclusion, it is argued that there may be a productivity gain if a member state decreases the tax burden in general (income taxes, social security contributions), and VAT rates in particular, in sectors where the role of *do-it-yourself work* and underground activities is significant[114] , and increases VAT rates in sectors where

---

113 Since the heavy tax burden on such services makes it expensive to buy them on the (formal) market, it is more attractive to make them yourself or buy them in the informal sector. See OECD (2011), Consumption Tax Trends 2010: VAT/GST and Excise Rates, Trends and Administration Issues, OECD Publishing, page 100.

114 This phenomenon of the black economy, understood as the set of economic activities which, although carried out on national territory, are not reflected in the product of the respective country, have no correspondence in national accounting and do not enter into the quantification of GDP, is a general concern for most EU member states. Some in particular, such as Belgium, Bulgaria, Greece, Hungary, Italy, Lithuania, Malta, Poland, Portugal, Romania, Slovenia and Spain, as well as Cyprus, face a special challenge in this area - European Commission, Taxation paper n° 34, "Tax

that role is demanding .[115]

As for the last two arguments, the promotion of certain goods in order to raise awareness and the favoring of poorer groups, they are based on the consideration that lower VAT rates on selected goods and services, mainly consumed by people on lower incomes, make such goods more accessible and ultimately generate a more equitable distribution of income. In fact, in many of the countries that apply reduced VAT rates, the introduction is traditionally justified by the assumption that the poorest families spend a significant part of their income on essential goods[116] . On the other hand, lower VAT rates on sorted goods and services (merit goods) can boost consumption of such goods by lowering their price, making them accessible to the lower-income population. In some cases, the selection of *favored* goods can alert consciences to more careful consumption, for example, favoring healthy foods, preferring more energy-efficient appliances and appliances in general, which in turn will have an effect on health costs and environmental wear and tear.

This issue of changing individual behavior is relevant because the level of VAT rates, by its very mechanism, can only have an impact on purchases made by final consumers. It will indirectly affect the behavior of companies through changes in consumer behavior.

5.1 GOODS AND SERVICES SUBJECT TO EXEMPTION/ZERO RATE VAT/REDUCED RATE VAT

The categories in which, as a rule and in most countries, reduced rates apply are as follows: a) essential goods such as medical and hospital services, food and water supplies; b) certain activities traditionally considered to be utilities (transport services, public postal and television services); c) activities considered socially desirable (cultural services, sports), or which promote local employment; d)

Reforms in EU Member States, Tax policy challenges for economic growth and fiscal sustainability", 2012, page 75.

115 In the report "Study on reduced VAT applied to goods and services in the Member States of the European Union", dated June 21, 2007, Copenhagen Economics contrasts doing housework or small repairs at home with producing one's own computer, to point out that the latter is one of the sectors where the role of do-it-yourself work is less expressive since its realization requires a degree of qualification that makes it less appealing for self-production.

116 COPENHAGEN ECONOMICS, op. cit., page 73, analyzing the European scenario, states that lower-income families spend around 20% of their income on food, while higher-income families spend only 12%.

geographical areas considered to deserve special treatment (islands, territories far from urban areas).

Let's take a look at some specific examples of goods and services, as well as the reasons given for this special treatment regime.

5.1.1 FOOD

When it comes to food goods/services, there is a strong inclination to exempt or tax at a lower rate. The question we can ask is whether all foodstuffs should be exempt or subject to a lower rate or, on the contrary, whether we should select which goods benefit from this. Here, the delimitation *of boundaries (boderlines)* within the same category of goods - food - is extremely important.

The assumption behind the exemption is that families on lower incomes do not have access to what are considered luxury foods. From the outset, it is necessary to define the so-called *essential goods* and *luxury goods.* In this regard, it seems to us that we can question whether the legislature should not itself define what some are and what others are. This is because of the obvious difficulty in defining these boundaries and in an attempt to reduce the subjectivity associated with the nature of that definition. The legislation ends up making this definition by establishing different lists (and different rates) for VAT. But the question that arises, in our view, is whether these lists and the way they are drawn up are based solely on social reasons, concerns about food, for example, which people should take care of and prioritize, rather than concerns about raising revenue.

In our case, the solution has been to define, in a list, what is subject to a lower tax. The lists are drawn up on the assumption that the foods considered basic for a healthy life must be accessible to everyone. Taxed at a reduced rate, taxation does not mean inaccessibility. Listing such goods based on this assumption can lead to some inconsistencies when confronted with the behavior of private individuals. Let's see, from a nutritional point of view, the consumption of fresh food is desirable and should therefore be exempt or subject to a reduced rate. However, today's families have less flexible schedules and, due to the volume and rush of their employers' work, they may prefer to buy and consume canned goods and ready-to-eat frozen dishes.

It is in this context that we can advocate taxing most foodstuffs, possibly at a lower rate, but accepting or agreeing to some exemptions, particularly for lower-income families.

The issue of exemptions can be dangerous and can even lead to a sequence of exemptions[117] , which will create more complexity in the structure of the tax. In the Portuguese case, a wide variety of goods and food products benefited from reduced tax rates. In recent years, especially since 2010, Lists I and II annexed to the CIVA have undergone significant changes and repeals, with the result that a large part of the food range included therein has gone from being taxed at reduced rates to being taxed at the standard rate. This was particularly true of the products that were part of list II (13% rate), since with LOE 2012 alone, fifteen items were repealed and the products moved to the 23% rate .[118]

5.1.2 ELECTRICITY AND GAS

Today, there is a more or less unanimous tendency to tax this type of service, but there were times when it was allowed and commonplace to benefit from it.

One of the arguments used in favor of taxation is the fact that the consumption of these goods is proportional to household income, i.e. as income increases, so does the consumption of these goods. On the other hand, there is the fact that these services are generally provided by the public service and if they were exempted

---

117 For example, as Alan Tait (1988) points out, Costa Rica wanted to exempt the consumption of ice cream and exempt ice cream producers. These, in turn, lobbied to exempt those who produce the machines that make the ice cream, who lobbied for an exemption on the handles and components (inputs) they use in the machines they produce.

118 Among the products that used to be taxed at 13% and are now taxed at 23 are nuts and dried fruit, whether or not in shell; directly edible oils and mixtures thereof (edible oils); margarines of animal and vegetable origin; products prepared from meat, fish, vegetables or horticultural products, stuffed pasta, pizzas, sandwiches and soups, even if presented in a frozen or pre-frozen state and ready-to-eat meals, in the ready-to-eat and take-away or home delivery systems; and, in terms of the provision of services, the provision of food and drink services.

there would be an increase in use by users, sometimes even unnecessary and misdirected. A question of fiscal coherence arises here: does it make sense to allow, on the one hand, a reduced rate on electricity and natural gas, if we assume that this will encourage consumption, when, on the other hand, what we want is to reduce it by promoting energy-saving materials and energy-efficient products, which are subject to a standardized rate?[119] Now, this argument is closely related to the issue we are discussing here of modeling behavior, since taxation is seen as a way of restricting the use, or at least the misuse, of those goods. This is, of course, on the assumption that an increase in taxation leads to a reduction, or at least moderation, in consumption.

The fact that it is provided by the public service, combined with the fact that it is usually concentrated in a few suppliers, makes it easier and more efficient to collect and administer the tax collected.

In the Portuguese case, Law No. 51-A/2011 of September 30 eliminated the reduced VAT rate on electricity and natural gas, with the consequent subjection of these goods to the standard rate .[120][121][122]

Arguing that energy policy calls for greater competitiveness, price transparency, proper functioning and effective liberalization of energy markets, Decree-Law 101/2011 of 30 September simultaneously justifies the need to *"adopt measures that guarantee access to these essential services for all consumers, particularly the economically vulnerable, regardless of their provider"*. In fulfillment of this objective, it created the **social tariff** for the natural gas sector. The social tariff for electricity was established by Decree-Law 138-A/2010 of December 28[121][122] . The pursuit of these objectives stems from the European Union's Third Energy

---

119 COM (2007), op. cit.

120 It repealed items 2.12 and 2.16 of list I annexed to the CIVA, with effect from October 1, 2011. In addition to the repeal of these items, and closely related to the sector, Article 123(2) of Law 64-B/2011 of December 30 repealed item 2.4 of list II annexed to CIVA, with such products (related to renewable energies) now being subject to the standard rate.

121 Complemented by ordinance no. 1334/2010, of December 31.

122 The aim of these social tariffs is to protect the interests of economically vulnerable end customers, i.e. those who benefit from: a) the solidarity supplement for the elderly; b) the social insertion income; c) the social unemployment allowance; d) the first scale of family allowance; e) the social invalidity pension.

Package[123] which, by establishing common rules for the internal markets in natural gas and electricity, requires the adoption of measures to protect vulnerable consumers.

In a context such as the current one, where the price of these goods and services is rising, as a result of the measures adopted to consolidate public accounts and relaunch the national economy, Decree-Law 102/2011 of September 30 creates the ASECE - **Extraordinary Social Support for Energy Consumers** .[124]

An interesting question will be to assess whether the compensation awarded by the mechanisms we have described is sufficient to "numb" the aggravating effect on those recipients.

5.1.3 MERIT GOODS

It is often said that there is a set of goods that should be exempt from tax because they are considered to be goods of merit[125][126] , which everyone should tend to consume regardless of their income and preferences. The Sixth Directive recognizes postal services, hospitals, medical services, education, cultural activities, public radio and television as activities of "public interest". These goods are usually provided by public entities and financed by taxes. The public provision of these goods, considered essential, is part of a logic in which the public sector

---

123 Parliament and Council Directives 2009/72/EC and 2009/73/EC of July 13.

124 The ASECE is calculated by applying a percentage discount to the electricity bill and natural gas bill of eligible final consumers and can be combined with the social tariffs for electricity and natural gas. Ministerial Order No. 275-A/2011, of September 30, set that percentage at 13.8% and stated that the discount "applies to the value of energy consumption and fixed terms or power of electricity and natural gas, net of other discounts, excluding VAT, other taxes, contributions, fees and interest on arrears that may apply". Ministerial Order 275-B/2011, of September 30, lays down a set of rules governing the procedures for awarding, maintaining and monitoring the ASECE. This support is aimed at natural persons who are in a position to benefit from the electricity or natural gas social tariff scheme and aims to ensure mechanisms to protect economically vulnerable end consumers in the face of the situation of increasing and volatile energy costs.

125 Merit goods are often related to "the essential values of the community, in which it imposes on citizens what it believes is best for them. (...) Society wants these goods to be provided, because merit goods contemplate something more than the sum of individual preferences, expressing collective values that are imposed on individuals. (...) They are above individual decisions and become a condition for coexistence in a given society.", Cruz, Neves Jose, Economia e Politica: uma abordagem dialectica da escolha publica, Coimbra Editora, 2008, page 49.

126 "The free, or tendentially free, provision of goods classified as meritorious (namely health and education) is an indispensable component of individual and social well-being and provides another rationale for public intervention in the field of social justice, beyond the distribution of income", Pereira, Paulo Trigo; Afonso, Antonio; Arcanjo, Manuela; Santos, Jose, Economia e Finangas Publicas, Escolar Editora, 2ª Edition, 2006, page 71 and 72.

carries out *"positive discrimination in the sense of equal opportunities and the potential better performance of those who, due to the misfortune of birth, health, territory, or other factors, would initially be worse placed to enjoy the advantages of the market"'.[2]*

These so-called merit goods are associated with the idea of an almost obligatory exemption. Let's look specifically at some of these goods .[127]

5.1.3.1 CHILDREN'S CLOTHING

There are countries that consider that this type of clothing should be exempt or zero-rated, on the assumption that it can represent a greater share of low-income families. The argument seems more emotional[128] than rational. First of all, there is no element in the composition of children's clothing and adult clothing that is exclusive to children's clothing. On the other hand, the proportion of expenditure on clothing and footwear in total household expenditure most often increases as household expenditure, and therefore income, increases.

Although it can't be considered children's clothing, but a hygiene product, it seems interesting to mention the case of children's diapers. In terms of VAT and in the Portuguese case, there was a time when a distinction was made between diapers for babies and diapers for adults with incontinence. The former would be a hygiene product, the latter a health, pharmaceutical or similar product. The former are taxed at the standard rate, the latter at the reduced rate[129] . The 2005 state budget law[130] , amended the sum under analysis by deleting the expression "for adults intended for incontinence", which meant that diapers (baby and adult) were treated similarly, i.e. both subject to the reduced rate[131][132] . This treatment is still maintained today, with

---

127 In this regard, we closely follow the examples of Alan Tait, op. cit.

128 "The emotional feeling that to tax children's clothing is more "immoral" than taxing old people's clothing or sick people's clothing.", TAIT, ALAN, op. Cit.

129 See list I annexed to the CIVA, item 2.4, which only referred to "adult pads and diapers for incontinents", in force since 24-03-92.

130 Law no. 55-B/2004, of December 30th.

131 As a result of this change, families who spend a lot on baby diapers saw their tax cut from 19 to 5%.

132 According to item 2.5 (because the previous item 2.4 was renumbered by Article 6 of Decree-Law 102/2008, of June

diapers in general being subject to the reduced rate of 6% .[132][133]

This raises the question of whether baby diapers should be treated in the same way as adult diapers. The states[133][134] that have opted to apply reduced rates argue, in addition to the reasons mentioned above, that there is no difference between the two, apart from the user.

Let's see, baby diapers are a necessity whose demand is determined by the number of children. A family buys as many diapers as they need for the hygiene and comfort of their child and for as long as the child needs them. No matter how cheap or expensive, you won't buy more or less than you need. Demand will be shaped by the number of children, not by the nail[135] . Reducing the cost of diapers by applying a reduced rate instead of the standard rate will not contribute to an increase in the fertility rate, since the higher or lower price of diapers will hardly factor into family planning decisions (as if this were the only *cost of* having a child!). The greater accessibility of diapers will not lead to more demand, because as we said, purchases will be made according to (temporary and variable) needs.

However, the argument that the cost of diapers can be a considerable expense in the budget of lower-income families with small children has some sustainability. The fact is that, instead of being subject to the reduced rate, it may be possible to opt for a direct transfer to the neediest families. The same prescription applies to adult

20) of List I annexed to the CIVA, which states that "this item includes diapers and diaper covers". See the binding information from the Tax Administration, referring to case no. 1083 and in the course of a request for clarification on Value Added Tax on printed and dyed diapers: "In accordance with the understanding of this Directorate of
Services, the supply of "diapers", whether disposable or not, and regardless of the material used to make them, fall under item 2.5 of List I annexed to the VAT Code", available at http://info.portaldasfinancas.gov.pt/NR/rdonlyres/655D2CB7-C79E-478B-.
987AEA4F9780EFAE/0/INFORMA
% C3%87%C3%83O.1083.pdf.
133 Diapers are not on the list of goods that the Commission has allowed to be subject to lower VAT rates (Council Directive 2006/112/EC of November 28, 2006, as amended by Directive 2009/47/EC). And, in fact, as soon as Portugal, through the LOE for 2005, transferred baby diapers from the normal rate to the reduced rate, voices in the Union protested against this conduct, and there were even infringement proceedings. The justification for the reduction and the lower rate was (and still is) to protect families with children, some of whom have several children wearing diapers. The government wanted to show some sensitivity towards these families and their costs.
134 Portugal, Hungary, Poland, Ireland and the United Kingdom, through agreements with the EU, apply special treatment to baby diapers, subjecting them to a zero tax rate just like other baby items such as clothes and shoes.
135 COPENHAGEN ECONOMICS, "Study on reduced VAT applied to goods and services in the Member States of the European Union", June 21, 2007, page 79.

diapers, since subjecting them to the standard rate would avoid the conflict of classification between adult and baby diapers. As for adults, a system for reimbursing the costs of medical prescriptions for diapers could be more efficient [136][137][138]

5.1.3.2 MEDICAL AND VETERINARY SERVICES

Article 13 of the Sixth Directive states that the provision of assistance services carried out in the exercise of medical and paramedical activities, as defined by the member state concerned[137] , must be exempt. We can have services such as SPAs, massages, which in some countries are considered medical activities and therefore exempt, and states that do not consider them so, since the definition is left up to each member state[138]. The choice of exemption or zero-rating inevitably brings with it a problem of qualification: knowing which services or goods should be considered meritorious to the point of being excluded from taxation. Qualification in itself can lead to excessive use of these services by those who are able to pay and those who are not. There could be overconsumption of the good, since consumers are not paying the true cost to society of producing the good[139] , and there may even be consumers who only consume it because it is "free". However, given that these services can be provided by public bodies, this would imply an increase in public spending on these services. On the other hand, it could be argued against the

---

136 Ibid.

137 Article 13(c).

138 With regard to the concept of providing medical services, the ECJ ruling of September 14, 2000, Case 384/98, considers such services to consist of providing assistance to people, diagnosing and treating a disease or any health anomaly. As far as paramedical activities are concerned, we have to resort to Decree-Law No. 261/93 of July 24 and Decree-Law No. 320/99 of August 11, which contain the requirements to be met in order to carry out the respective activities. According to these laws, the exercise of these activities includes the use of scientifically-based techniques for the purposes of health promotion and disease prevention, diagnosis and treatment, or rehabilitation.

See the binding information issued by the AT in case no. 1276: "In the specific case, and taking into account the concept of providing medical or paramedical services, it appears that lymphatic drainage treatments cannot benefit from the exemption provided for in art. 9 of CIVA, and are subject to taxation at the normal rate provided for in art. 18 of CIVA, available at http://info.portaldasfinancas.gov.pt/NR/rdonlyres/48AFBC2E-521B-460C-BBF7-44FF2F8F77A0 /0/INFORMA %C3%87%C3%83O.1276.pdf .

139 "The use of administrative or political prices below market prices is reflected in an inefficient allocation of resources, in which too many resources are invested in a given sector, to the detriment of applications in other sectors." PEREIRA, PAULO TRIGO; AFONSO, ANTONIO; ARCANJO, MANUELA; SANTOS, JOSE, Economia e Finangas Publicas, Escolar Editora, 2ª Edition, 2006, page 74.

exemption[140] that if the aim is to help a group of people who, either because of their low income, have no way of accessing health services other than free, or because of their illness are forced to spend large sums on services of this kind, direct help and assistance from the state would be more efficient.

There are other situations that are generally not considered to be worthy of exempting the respective goods and services, such as veterinary services[141] , because they are not extensions of medical services. These services, when used by private individuals and for private purposes, of which pets are an example, are taxed at the normal rate. However, if we are talking about animals and veterinary services that are real *inputs* for farmers, these services may benefit from an exemption, especially in countries where agriculture is an important source of income. However, Community guidance on this matter is clear in that it does not consider them to be "as meritorious" as medical services and as such they should be subject to VAT .[142]

In our case, the provision of services carried out within the scope of veterinary medicine was exempt from VAT under Article 9(1)(c) of the Value Added Tax Code[143] , in its original wording. This exemption was repealed by Law 30-C/92 of December 28. As a result, VAT now applies to all medical and veterinary services provided from January 7, 1993[144] , whether these services are provided in the context of agriculture or to pets, and regardless of whether they are provided by natural or legal persons.

In terms of Community law, these services were provided for in paragraph 2 of

---

140 Note that when we talk about exemption, we are referring to an exemption of services and goods for everyone, whether or not they have the ability to pay.

141 See the AT's binding information, regarding case no. 1147, following a request from a company dedicated to hotel accommodation for animals, for inclusion in list I of the CIVA, similar to the inclusion enjoyed by similar services provided to humans, which considers that the activity does not fall under item 2.17 of List I, nor in any other list annexed to the CIVA, so that these services are subject to VAT at the normal rate in force, available at http://info.portaldasfinancas.gov.pt/NR/rdonlyres/C6A2269D-1F7D-4A6F-BDDF-CB68C272E263/0/ INFORMA%C3%87%C3%83O.1147.pdf.

142 The discretion granted by the Community to some states was solely because those same states had not previously taxed those services.

143 Approved by DL. No. 394-A/84, of December 26.

144 Date on which the legal amendment came into force.

Annex F of the Sixth Directive, which contained the activities that had to be taxed for VAT purposes. There was, however, the possibility of exempting such activities, but only for a transitional period of five years[145] . The Sixth Directive was repealed by Council Directive 2006/112/EC, which did not introduce any changes in this area.

Having said that, it can be concluded that the provision of services in the exercise of the profession of veterinary surgeon does not qualify for exemption from VAT .[146]

5.1.3.3   *CULTURAL ACTIVITIES*

There is also the widespread idea that cultural activities are worthy enough to be VAT-free. Of the more specific areas we've dealt with, this will be the one that generates the most room for differing opinions. This is because what for some is considered culture for others may be a waste of money'. The representation of what it is and the feeling it provokes in the spectator differs from person to person. There are those who love an opera show and are willing to pay a large sum to see it; there

---

145 Article 28(4).

146 This prohibition derives not only from an option of the national legislator, but from Community law itself. One question that arises is whether, as a result of the addition of item 4.2 to list I (reduced rate) annexed to the CIVA by Law 66-B/2012, of December 31, the State Budget Law for 2013, the provision of veterinary medical services in the field of animals assigned to agricultural holdings can be understood to fall within its scope. In terms of EU law, there is no express reference to it in paragraph 11 of Annex III of the VAT Directive, which makes it impossible to fill in any gaps. On the other hand, the provision of services is not expressly provided for in any of the sections of item 4.2 of list I annexed to the CIVA. However, as we have already mentioned, items 4.2 (a) to (i) do not constitute a numerus clausus, and it is possible for other services not included therein to benefit from a tax reduction, provided that they contribute to the general purpose of agricultural production. The answer, then, will be whether the services provided in the exercise of the profession of veterinary surgeon in the field of agriculture contribute to the realization of agricultural production, under the terms of section 4.2 and paragraph 11 of Annex III of the VAT Directive. If this is the case, they can benefit from the reduced VAT rate.

On the other hand, it has been understood that transfers of medicinal products for exclusive use in human medicine, medicinal products for exclusive use in veterinary medicine and medicinal products for use in both areas fall within the scope of point a) of item 2.5 of list I annexed to the VAT Code, although other products for human or animal use not included in the concept of "medicinal products, pharmaceutical specialties and other pharmaceutical products intended exclusively for therapeutic and prophylactic purposes" are not. It is therefore understood that the possibility of applying a reduced VAT rate provided for in point 3) of Annex III of the VAT Directive (2006/112/EC) also includes exclusively veterinary medicines. On this point, see the AT's binding information in case no. 1028: "If veterinary doctors or veterinary clinics, when carrying out their services with the application of medicines, indicate separately, on the corresponding invoice, the operations carried out (provision of services and supply of medicines), the respective taxation must be done at the rate corresponding to each; in other words, they must apply the normal rate to the provision of services and the reduced rate to the supply of medicines. However, if this separation is not shown on the invoice, the medicines should be considered to be included in the provision of services and the standard rate should be applied", information available at

are those who refuse an offered ticket. In fact, the value of the term "Culture" lies in the satisfaction that each person derives from the object that calls itself cultural.

As this is a concept full of subjectivity, it will certainly not be easy to list cultural activities for the purposes of exemption. For this reason, there are those who argue that the best bet would not be to exempt all cultural activities, but rather to subject cultural activities to the standard rate and to provide direct aid, through subsidies for example, to specific activities. Of course, once again there is the difficulty of justifying the allocation to just one group or activity. For example, those in political power could want to benefit lower-income households by facilitating their access to cultural goods and services. However, it could be that certain families, because they don't have "cultural habits", because they have a tradition of poverty that has always prevented them from enjoying shows of this kind, or because they come from geographical areas with fewer cultural offerings, even with the privileges granted, don't prefer such goods.

As far as publications are concerned, any solution proposed will be subjective, because what we said above applies. It will always be difficult to justify why one publication or type of publication is more important than another. The solution adopted will always depend on the political choice of whoever has to make it at the time. To avoid the possibility of changes depending on the political orientation of those who are[147] called upon to govern and legislate, one way would be to subject all publications to the same VAT rate. In our country, periodicals and books are subject to 6%[148] . The point is that if we do this, we won't be using VAT to shape behavior. We're not encouraging reading. Not only are we not inciting the right behavior, but we could also direct the public towards less correct and even illegal

http://info.portaldasfinancas.gov.pt/NR/rdonlyres/84B15603D008404EA7A467C914DF63E9/0/INFORMA%C3%87%C3%83O.1028.pdf.

147 Alan Tait, op. cit. page 72
148 Heading 2.1, in the version of Law no.º 55-A/2010, of December 31, with the exception of publications or books of an obscene or pornographic nature, considered as such in the relevant legislation, and works bound in leather, silk or similar fabrics. Item 2.4 (Books, pamphlets and other non-periodical publications of a cultural, educational, recreational or sporting nature, in paperback or bound) was repealed by Law 55-A/2010 of December 31, and is now taxed at the standard rate.

behavior. To what extent can we associate the spread of illegal copying of music, films and books with the rise in VAT rates and the consequent increase in nails? Aren't these occurrences the result of people choosing alternative ways of accessing their favorite goods?[149]

---

149 COPENHAGEN ECONOMICS, op. cit., page 82, discusses the case of Sweden, which lowered the VAT rate on books in 2002. It is noted that Sweden applied a rate of 25% to books, while the rate applied to newspapers and cultural events was 6%. Because of the high VAT rate, books appeared to consumers to be more expensive than other cultural goods. In the face of this, the internet made it possible to buy cheaper books in other countries that applied lower VAT rates; small bookstores, located in more remote areas, were considered particularly affected, leading the state to distribute subsidies (more than 10 million in 2002). The lowering of VAT in Sweden was implemented to lower prices and increase sales, in order to promote reading, book quality and variety of content. In 2002 the decision was made to lower the VAT rate on books to 6%. The drop in VAT was immediately reflected in the drop in nails. In the year following the VAT cut, book sales increased by 16%, and this trend continued with 2005 becoming known as the bumper year. The VAT cut was akin to a sectoral subsidy, with the state losing more than 600 million in tax revenue. The greater volume of business seems to have eliminated the need for and dependence on subsidies on the part of bookshops located in more remote regions and, at the same time, brought a large number of small publishers into the market, specializing in quality or niche content. However, apart from the increase in sales, there are no conclusive results that reading has been boosted or increased. The evidence shows, in fact, that low prices do not increase reading by those (or among those) who no longer want or feel like reading.

6. THE PROBLEM

Almost across the board, VAT is a preferred tax. Especially when the purpose of its imposition is to raise revenue. The characteristic of neutrality and the "numbing" effect on consumption lead to this preference. Some even claim that *"VAT is the most effective instrument for generating government revenue[150] "*. In the words of Sergio Vasques (2005), *"it is quite simply the most formidable fiscal creature ever conceived"*. The reasons given are as follows: of all the taxes, VAT is the most productive, covering in principle all transactions of goods and services; it is the most economical, shifting the costs of management and policing from the administration to the taxpayer; it is the most neutral, both in terms of internal trade and international trade .[151]

In the EU context[152] , between 2011 and 2012, many Member States made changes to VAT in order to increase tax revenue. Most of them raised the standard VAT rate. In Portugal, as we have already mentioned, from January 2011, the standard rate was increased by two percentage points to 23%, three points higher than its level in June 2010. The United Kingdom, after a temporary reduction to 15% in 2009, raised the standard rate from 17.5% to 20% in January 2011. In 2012, Cyprus and Ireland increased their standard rates by two percentage points, to 17% and 23% respectively. Since January 1, 2012, Hungary has had the highest standard rate in the EU, at 27% (seven points higher than in 2009). Countries such as Latvia, Poland, Slovakia and Italy increased their rates by 1% in 2011. Italy increased its standard VAT rate by 2% to 23%. All these changes meant that the average standard VAT rate in the EU-27 rose progressively from 19.8% in 2009 to 21% in

---

150 GO, DELFIN S., KEARNEY MARNA, ROBINSON SHERMAN, and THIERFELDER KAREN, "An Analysis of South Africa's Value Added Tax", World Bank Plocy Research Working Paper N° 3671, 2005, p. 19, quoted in "An International Perspective on VAT" by Alain Charlet and Jeffrey Owens in TAX NOTES INTERNATIONAL, N° 12, September 2010, p. 944.

151 VASQUES, SERGIO, "Origem e Finalidades dos Impostos Especiais de Consumo", RFDT, Belo Horizonte, year 3, no. 17, pages 49-98, Sept/Oct 2005.

152 EUROPEAN COMMISSION, Taxation paper n° 34, "Tax Reforms in EU Member States, Tax policy challenges for economic growth and fiscal sustainability", 2012, page 119.

2012. In the three-year period 2010-2012, almost half of the Member States increased the standard and/or reduced rate in order to increase revenue. In several countries, the rate was increased[153] , while others opted to broaden the scope of VAT by repealing exemptions[154] and reducing the scope of existing reduced rates (notably Portugal).

Most of these changes were aimed at increasing tax revenue. In exceptional cases, some states have opted (in some cases temporarily) for a reduction in the tax burden for specific goods and services, moving them to the lowest rates[155] . These changes are justified not only for reasons of distribution (reduced rates for goods such as food or merit goods), but also because of concerns about economic developments in specific sectors (e.g. construction).

Outside the European Union, countries such as Iceland, Mexico, New Zealand and Sweden have also increased VAT rates. There are big differences in rates between OECD countries, ranging from 5% in Japan and Canada, to 25% in Denmark, Iceland, Norway and Sweden, and 27% in Hungary.

In the general context of the economic crisis we are going through, tax management as a whole tends to be at the forefront of the political debate. The watchword is "AUSTERITY" and, although this means strict control of spending, it is accompanied by a harsh increase in the tax burden. Given the current scenario, the maintenance/cutting of salaries, rising unemployment rates, social security contribution rates that are likely to decline as a result of rising unemployment and low salaries, it may be that the increase in the tax burden on the income sector does not correspond to an increase in revenue for the state. This is where VAT comes in as the "preferred" tax, as it may be less affected, since consumption will always have to exist, although revenue may be reduced as a result of the fall in consumption, also due to the fall in wages and disposable income.

---

153 As in Latvia, Poland, France, Bulgaria (where the reduced rates apply only to tourist services), Greece, and, in 2012, the Czech Republic, where there was an increase from 10 to 14%.
154 For example, Cyprus, Belgium, Denmark, Finland.
155 Belgium, Cyprus, Greece, Spain and Sweden.

With VAT in the spotlight[156] , there is one element to consider as a problem: the number of different rates implemented in various countries. In fact, this is a hotly debated topic that doesn't appear to be closed in the short term .[157]

Alain Charlet and Jeffrey Owens (2010) discuss this problem: the existence of multiple VAT rates will affect the efficiency of the VAT system, as it implements complexity, which will translate into increased administrative and *compliance* costs.

According to these authors, it is possible to identify two groups of countries: countries that have introduced VAT systems based on the French and European model and countries that have implemented a different VAT system. The first group of countries (most of which are members of the EU) generally apply various reduced rates, so that the calculation base and incidence subject to the standard rate is somewhat limited[158] . In line with these authors, they also point out that the main reason for applying reduced rates in Europe is the concern to relieve taxes on goods and services that represent a greater expense in the households of poorer families. We'll come back to this later.

The second group[159] has a broader base at the standard rate, although sometimes accompanied by the zero-rating of some goods and services. However, these countries have a single rate lower than most standard rates applied in EU member states and lower than the 15% minimum determined by the VAT directive .[160]

---

156 "The recent financial and economic crises have pushed a number of governments to increase their standard VAT rates as a means of reducing deficits and this trend may continue." OECD (2011), Consumption Tax Trends 2010: VAT/GST and Excise Rates, Trends and Administration Issues, OECD Publishing, page 75

157 Taxation paper no. 2, VAT Indicators, Mathis, Alexandre, April 2004, pp. 4 and 8, available at http://ec.europa.eu/taxation_customs/resources/documents/vat_indicators.pdf, states that in 2000, taking into account the EU-15 average, 69% of transactions subject to VAT were taxed at the standard rate; however, in some member states (including Portugal) the percentage of transactions subject to that rate was lower than the European average and in some below 50% (Ireland, Luxembourg and Spain). It can therefore be concluded that reduced rates are not as much of an exception as they should be.

158 According to what we explained in chapter two, point 2.1, Council Directive 2006/112/EC of November 28 allows EU member states to have a standard rate that cannot be lower than 15% and two reduced rates that cannot be lower than 5%. On the other hand, we have also seen that it allows older member states "reserved rights", according to which they can continue to apply the reduced rate below the minimum indicated in the directive, as long as that rate has been in force since before 1991.

159 Including Australia, Canada, Korea, New Zealand, South Africa, Singapore.

160 Take the case of the rates in Australia (10% since it implemented VAT in 2000 and which have remained

A European study comparing actual VAT revenue with the revenue that would be obtained if all private consumption were taxed at the standard rate and the revenue were actually collected has signaled a number of countries that must substantially improve the design and structure of VAT in order to increase its efficiency[161][162] . This tax efficiency crisis is often blamed on the impact of the use of exemptions and reduced rates. It is said to be a problem of "political efficiency". Other factors, such as tax evasion and non-compliance, a matter of "collection efficiency", contribute to these results.

In fact, one of the EU's priorities is to make the VAT system more effective, efficient and equitable. As Clotilde Celorico Palma (2012) points out[162] , there is a general feeling that the fragmentation of the VAT system into 27 national systems is the main obstacle to effective intra-EU trade, as it prevents citizens from enjoying the benefits of a true single market. Speaking of internationally active companies, they consider that the effective price they pay for weak and insufficient harmonization results in complexity, extra compliance costs and legal uncertainty. On the other hand, SMEs do not always have the necessary resources to deal with this situation and, because of this, they may even refrain from participating in cross-border activities, damaging/limiting their *performance[163][16]* ^.

6.1 ARGUMENTS IN FAVOR OF A SINGLE TAX

The studies that have been carried out on this matter suggest that a broader base and a single VAT rate is preferable, since the current VAT rate structure is *merely the result of past political negotiations[163][164][165]* . This point of view is supported by

---

unchanged), Canada (7% since 1992 and which fell to 6% in 2007 and 5% in 2008) and New Zealand (10% since 1988, rising in 1990 to 12.5% and to 15% in 2011), countries which do not apply reduced rates. OECD (2012), Consumption Tax Trends 2012: VAT/GST and Excise Rates, Trends and Administration Issues, OECD Publishing, page 69.

161 Greece, Italy, Spain, Latvia, Romania, United Kingdom, Slovakia, Portugal, France, Belgium, Ireland, Poland and Lithuania, EUROPEAN COMMISSION, Taxation Paper n° 34, op. Cit. Pag. 72.

162 PALMA, CELORICO CLOTILDE, "The Commission's recent communication on the future of VAT", TOC Magazine no. 144, March 2012.

163 The National Statistics Institute, in a study published on June 29, 2012 and available at: http://www.ine.pt/xportal/xmain?xpid=INE&xpgid=ine_destaques&DESTAQUESdest_boui=133411720&D ESTAQUESmodo=2, concludes that in 2010 Portuguese micro, small and medium-sized enterprises (SMEs) represented

recent studies[166] which claim that a broad base with a single rate would allow for higher revenues on the one hand and, on the other hand, lower tax costs for the Tax Administration, as well as lower implementation costs for businesses[167] . Ultimately, the result could be the application of a standard rate lower than those currently applicable in countries that have several VAT rates .[168]

These arguments are generally supported by the view that VAT is not an appropriate instrument for manipulating social behavior .[169]

Another argument against a VAT structure with multiple rates and exemptions is that it creates complexity and will therefore be more difficult for taxpayers to comply with and for revenue bodies to administer[170] . This complexity can also result in legal uncertainty. This is because similar products may be subject to a standard rate or a minimum rate depending on the ingredients they contain. Let's look at an example from the UK of products containing potatoes: foods such as potato chips are subject to the standard rate, while cookies are subject to the zero rate[171] . Another example: teacakes with chocolate icing are subject to the standard

---

99.9% of the Portuguese business fabric, but accounted for less than two-thirds (60.9%) of the turnover of the Portuguese business sector.

164 The issue of "collection efficiency" is a concern within the European Union. A robust and fraud-proof VAT system is called for, requiring that modern VAT collection and control methods maximize the revenue actually collected and, as a result, limit fraud and evasion. This will require national tax authorities to focus on risky behavior and, ultimately, to act collectively as a European VAT authority. A rapid, intensified and automatic exchange of information between national tax administrations will be vital to achieving this goal, PALMA, CELORICO CLOTILDE, Idem.

165 COM (2007), op. cit.

166 COPENHAGEN ECONOMICS, "Study on Reduced VAT Applied to Goods and Services in the Member States of the European Union", June 21, 2007, reproduced in Taxation Paper No. 13 of the European Commission of October 13, 2008; see also: OECD (2011), Consumption Tax Trends 2010: VAT/GST and Excise Rates, Trends and Administration Issues, OECD Publishing, page 15.

167 Of the twenty-eight EU member countries, only Denmark applies a flat rate (25%) of VAT.

168 As an example, see a study carried out in Sweden on the application of a standardized rate of VAT which concludes that such an application would mean a reduction in application costs of SEK 500 million (about 54 million euros), Report 2006:3B on the costs of applying VAT in Sweden, Skatteverket, available at http://skatteverket.se/omskatteverket/rapporter.4.584dfe11039cdb626980000.html.

169 "An International Perspective on VAT" by Alain Charlet and Jeffrey Owens in TAX NOTES INTERNATIONAL, N° 12, September 2010, p. 949. See also Taxation Paper n° 2, op. Cit., page 5 "... this tax is not intended to alter the type or the quantities of goods and services purchase by the consumer.

170 "Information Note- Developments in VAT Compliance Management in Selected Countries", OECD Forum on Tax Administration: Compliance Sub-Group, August 2009, available at http: //www. oecd.org/tax/ administration/43728444.pdf.

171 In the context of this issue, the "Pringles case" is suggestive. The issue was the classification of Pringles as a potato chip or as a kind of cookie. Depending on this classification, Pringles could be subject to standard

rate, normal cookies without chocolate icing are subject to the zero rate .[172]

All this difficulty in classifying goods and products can lead to problems between entrepreneurs and the authorities, especially when it comes to border cases. It can also open the door to fraud, particularly intentional misclassification of products .[173]

6.2 WHAT'S THE OPTION?

This issue of applying/opting for reduced VAT rates instead of a single standard rate has been discussed whenever a reform of consumption taxation is considered. However, the issue of reduced VAT rates is not conclusive174. In 2009, France lowered the VAT rate from 19.6% to 5.5% for restaurant and *catering* suppliers, on the assumption that this would result in a substantial reduction in employment, an increase in wages, or even the creation of new jobs and positions. According to the French National Institute of Statistics and Economic Studies (INSEE), restaurant prices fell by just 1.1% in July, 0.2% in August, 0.1% in September, and rose by 0.1% in October (2009). The same institute notes that only 30% of the VAT cuts were passed on to customers .[174][175]

---

rate (if they were considered potato chips) or zero rate (as a cookie). The High Court of Justice ruled in July 2008, in the course of an appeal against a 2007 decision of the VAT & Duties Tribunal, that Pringles cannot be considered to be made from potato since they contain only 42% potato; in order to be subject to tax the product must be made wholly or substantially from potato. The Court of Appeal disagreed in May 2009, finding that Pringles contained more than enough potato to be considered potato-based. Pringles are therefore subject to VAT at the standard rate. See Revenue & Customs Brief 32/09, May 2009, available at http://www.hmrc.gov.uk/briefs/vat/brief3209.htm; "Appeal Judges Decide Pingles Are Potato Crisps" The Telegraph, May 20, 2009, available at http://www.telegraph.co.uk/news/newstopics/politics/lawandorder/5355898/Appeal-judges-decide-Pringles- are-potato-crisps.html; Pilgrim, Robin, "Pringles Liable to UK VAT, Court Rules", LawAndTax-News.com, May 26, 2009, available at http://www.tax-.
news.com/news/pringles_liable_to_uk_vat_court_rules_36913.html;

172 See the judgment of the ECJ in Marks & Spencer plc v. Commissioners of Customs and Excise.
Excise, Case C-309/06, of April 10, 2008, available at:
http://curia.europa.eu/juris/document/document.jsf?text=&docid=71049&pageIndex=0&doclang=PT&mode
=lst&dir=&occ=first&part=1&cid=1049172

173 A study published by the EU Commission in 2009 shows that most VAT revenue is lost in the EU (more than 10 billion euros) as a result of evasion and fraud, "Study to Quantify and Analyse the VAT Gap in the EU-25 Member States", September 21, 2009, available at
http://ec.europa.eu/taxation_customs/resources/documents/taxation/tax_cooperation/combating_tax_fraud/re
ckon_report_sep2009.pdf, page 100.

174 In 2001, South Africa extended the zero tax rate to paraffin, a fuel widely used by the poorest families. However, this measure proved to be ineffective as the suppliers of this product absorbed most of the benefits and they were not passed on to consumers as intended, GO DELFIN S., KEARNEY MARNA, ROBINSON SHERMAN, and

The cut in VAT rates may, at least in theory, save jobs in the restaurant industry, which has been potentially affected by the economic crisis, but in practice it doesn't seem easy to quantify. Research into the reduced VAT rate granted to the hotel industry in Germany, as part of a tax cut to take effect from 2010, shows that it has not been passed on to consumers, as prices will have remained the same[176] . Once again, it seems that the main beneficiaries of the tax cut were the service providers, who invested the money saved by the tax in renovations or purchases.

In order to assess whether the effects of a cut in tax rates are passed on to the consumer or consumed by the producer and, on the other hand, whether they affect employment levels, it is also important to know the nature of the cut, i.e. whether it is prolonged or a temporary measure. This is because producers seem to be more willing to respond to changes in consumption tax rates in situations where those changes are *"here to stay"*. In fact, if they realize that the measure is temporary, they will be less willing to adjust their production capacity, hire more workers, invest in new machinery, since, as the change is temporary, so will be the increase in demand for their goods. If the tax returns to its previous state, demand will follow. What's more, the change in production and consequently in the price of goods may depend on costs that producers would necessarily have to bear. Costs that would exist and would be of equal value whether the change in VAT rates was *large or small.* In the case of a small change, producers may not change prices or they may take the opportunity to adjust prices much higher than those resulting from previous small adjustments they did not make.

On the other hand, we have already mentioned several times that one of the main arguments of member states that use a VAT structure with several rates (including reduced rates) is to reach lower-income families, making a range of goods and

---

THIERFELDER KAREN, "An Analysis of South africa's value Added Tax", World Bank Plocy Research Working Paper N° 3671, 2005, quoted in "An International Perspective on VAT" by Alain Charlet and Jeffrey Owens in TAX NOTES INTERNATIONAL, N° 12, September 2010, p. 950.
175 "Conjoncture frangaise", INSEE, December 2009, available at http://www.insee.fr/fr/themes/indicateur.asp?id=29.
176 LOMAS, ULRIKA, "German Hoteliers Fail to Pass On Vat Reduction", January 2010, Tax-
News.com, available at http://www.lawandtax-
news.com/asp/German_Hoteliers_Fail_to_pass_On_Vat_Reduction_41129.html.

services considered essential accessible to them. One of these goods is, in general, the food basket. However, this argument ignores the fact that wealthier families also benefit from the reduced rates, because they also consume the food basket, made up of goods on which the lowest tax rates apply. In fact, in general, the richest even consume more essential goods than the poor[177] , so the lower tax can be a relief for these consumers. The same applies to so-called *luxury goods.* It is assumed that reducing VAT rates increases demand. This refers to demand for merit goods (such as books, music, cultural events) but also goods with positive externalities such as energy-saving devices .[178][179]

In practice, this lower tax may not have the desired effect, as higher-income families may take advantage of the lower prices and buy more tickets to cultural events, for example[178][179][180] . Lower-income families may continue to be unable or unwilling to pay[181] . As for the consumption of more energy-efficient equipment, the result could be somewhat mixed, since it could both lead consumers to buy more energy-efficient equipment and, at the same time, lead consumers to use the same equipment more intensively. As the OECD (2011) points out "... *it is difficult to predict consumers' behavior and therefore ensure that the objectives of reduced VAT rates are met"[182]* .

Another consequence of lower taxes is the possibility of distorting consumer choices. Easier access to certain products can lead to overconsumption on the part of consumers and, consequently, to waste. In this way, consumers are adulterated by the different VAT rates[183] . In this sense, it is pointed out that the application of

---

177 "Policy Brief - Consumption Taxes: The Way of the Future", OECD Observer, October 2007.56
178 OEDC (2011), op. cit., page 98.
179 The Constitution of the Portuguese Republic requires the correction of positive externalities: the state is obliged to grant tax and financial benefits to cooperatives (art. 85), to support small and medium-sized enterprises (arts. 86 to 100), to promote scientific research and technological innovation (art. 73), to stimulate physical culture and sport (art. 79).
180 The application of reduced rates on some valuable goods such as books and music tends to create some tensions with the functioning of the internal market, mainly due to the ease of electronic commerce.
181 "Reduced VAT rates are generally not the most efficient way of redistributing income", "that consumption taxes are poor instruments for redistribution". European Commission, Taxation paper n° 34, "Tax Reforms in EU Member States, Tax policy challenges for economic growth and fiscal sustainability", 2012, pages 29 and 54 respectively.
182 OEDC (2011), op. cit., page 99.
183 Let's look at the following example: if it costs less to produce a pair of shoes than a sweater, but the VAT rate on the

uniform VAT rates will mean that all economic activities subject to VAT are treated in an equivalent way, which, from the consumer's perspective, will be eligible so as not to distort their choice.

Changes in prices due to different VAT rates can, however, have some positive effects on consumer choices, depending on the type of goods they affect. So, if we're talking about food, when the price of food goes up, for example due to a harmonization of VAT rates, it will be more natural for consumers to continue consuming those goods[184] , while having to reduce consumption of other goods considered non-essential.

The adoption and application of a differentiated VAT rate structure has another drawback, the so-called *compliance or application costs.* First of all, as mentioned above, it is difficult for the tax authorities to measure elasticities. In fact, they would have to be able to measure the price/income elasticity for each product, but also to regularly reassess that elasticity in line with consumer preferences (which may change, for example, with the introduction of new products on the market).

In other sectors, compliance costs are more visible, given the diversity of products, classes and subclasses. Often, as we have already mentioned, lower rates are the result of the legislator's attraction to the different treatment of healthier products, more efficient equipment, etc. However, this differentiation can create significant administrative costs, as reduced rates can create conflicts between traders, producers and the tax authorities, who are hungry for a low rate for their products[185] . These difficulties are visible in the delimitation of borderline cases.

---

sweater is so low that the sweater is cheaper than the shoes, then it induces the consumer to buy a sweater, whereas they would have preferred the shoes, which they are producing less expensively, Copenhagen Economics, op. cit, Similarly, if the VAT rate is lower for clothes than for books, for example, the consumer may be induced to buy a suitcase of clothes instead of a book, which by the way he was already tempted to buy. And it should be noted that the production costs of both products may even be the same and the consumer could, between the two with the same price, prefer the book, but the final price for the purchaser (lower on the clothes peg due to the lower tax rate) will be preponderant in the final choice and decision.

184 "Instead of going to bed hungry", COPENHAGEN ECONOMICS, op. cit. pp. 7 and 43.

185 Idem, page 77, and we are referred to the example of Ireland, which taxes cold pizza at a zero rate and hot pizza at 13.5% as take-away. Other examples we can mention: Waterfields (Leigh) Ltd v Revenue &

Customs [2008] UKVAT V20761 (06 August 2008), available at http://judgmental.org.uk/judgments/ UKVAT/2008/ [2008] _UKVAT_V20761.html, Ainsleys of Leeds Ltd v Revenue & Customs [2006] UKVAT V19694 (09 August

The structure of VAT has consequences for the functioning of the internal market and can alter the model of trade between member states .[186]

As stated in the Commission Communication of July 2007 consequent to the Copenhagen Economics final report, the implementation costs reflect the lack of harmonization of the rules: the more different rules are applied in the EU, the more companies have to spend to comply with the regulations in the various member states. A company that sells the same goods in all twenty-eight EU countries will have to invest in a detailed analysis of tax levels, as well as having to bear the administrative costs of the different VAT rules in the various member states. Even at national level, cross-border cases give rise to many problems of interpretation regarding the application of rates to products.

In conclusion, there seem to be strong arguments for making the VAT system simpler and more uniform. The simplification perspective combines aspects of VAT legislation (national and Community) with aspects relating to the performance of the tax administration (with a view to better coordination and cooperation between member states).

The conclusion we can draw is that there is no ideal VAT system. The structure and design of the tax will always depend on the economic, political, social and historical characteristics of the place in question, as well as on the level of revenue needed by the public sector to finance the public sector itself. Nevertheless, economic analysis suggests that VAT's greatest potential would be best achieved by broadening the tax base and eliminating reduced rates .[187]

2006), available at

http://judgmental.org.uk/judgments/UKVAT/2006/p006] _UKVAT_ V19694.html and The Lewis's Group Ltd V4931 available at http://www.hmrc.gov.uk/manuals/vfood manual/vfood4320.htm.

186 This concern is more pronounced in transactions involving goods and services that are more susceptible to distance selling, such as branded clothing, hand tools, books, CDs, DVDs, electronic equipment, and not so much in goods that are highly perishable, such as food. Taxation paper No. 13 of the European Commission, dated October 13, 2008, which reproduces the 2007 Copenhagen Economics Study.

187 OECD (2012), Consumption Tax Trends 2012: VAT/GST and Excise Rates, Trends and Administration Issues, OECD Publishing, page 66.

6.3 EXCISE DUTIES

An analysis of all the taxes we have in our legal system, and similar to other legal systems in general, shows that there is a range of products that are subject to a specific tax, which is generally heavier. Examples include tobacco, alcohol and alcoholic beverages, oil products, among others. These goods, on which excise duties (TECs) are levied from the outset, are considered to be harmful goods or to have unhealthy consequences, and their taxation is also justified for this reason. We also say this because the main objective of their imposition is to raise revenue (which is intrinsic to the nature of the tax).

Excise duties, then, can be aimed, in addition to revenue, at discouraging the consumption of certain products that are considered harmful. It has therefore been used as a means of influencing consumer behavior in various sectors (which is why we have given it its own chapter/space in our study).

The justification seems simple and logical: with regard to alcoholic beverages and tobacco, drinking and smoking are harmful to health, the tax levied is intended to reduce consumption habits by discouraging them; with regard to fuels, it is a mixture of concern for environmental health and the conservation of energy sources/resources.

But what is the point of changing consumer habits anyway?

The reason for the change has to be thought of not just in the immediate term, but as a kind of long-term investment. Let's see, if we can get people to stop smoking (or at least cut down on it), and switch to healthier foods, we'll have a higher percentage of healthy people and fewer obese children, for example. This issue of child education and children as a target group seems important to us because if they are brought up "from a young age" with good eating habits, they will more easily pass them on to their children and, in this way, we will guarantee healthier generations to come with more balanced habits[188] . If we control obesity, we will

---

188 The Portuguese Association Against Childhood Obesity warns, based on data from the World Health Organization,

reduce the costs inherent in hospital treatments (for example, hospitalizations for gastric banding), leaving hospitals and health facilities freer for other treatments with less "controllable" causes. The same goes for tobacco. We'll reduce the cost of follow-up appointments and potential lung cancer diagnoses, among other things[189] . Let's just say that the benefits would come in a chain, *one leading to another.*

The same reasons for preventing and dissuading behavior lead to internal distinctions being made in some products. For example, within the large group of tobacco products, countries choose to differentiate between those that are less harmful, in order to divert consumers towards the *less harmful habit.* Cigarettes, for example, are taxed at a higher rate than so-called "rolling tobacco", because the concentration of harmful substances is higher in the former .[190]

The truth is, the data on deaths caused by these evildoers is frightening![191] . According to 2011 data, the main causes of death in Portugal are diseases of the circulatory system (30.7%), malignant tumors (24.85%) and diseases of the respiratory system (11.6%)[192] . These causes are associated with risk factors that increase them, such as smoking, obesity, a sedentary lifestyle, careless eating and alcohol consumption. With this in mind, there are growing efforts to reduce them by promoting healthier lifestyles.

Could one of the ways of promoting a healthier lifestyle be through taxation? Better

---

that one in three children in Portugal is overweight or obese; according to the European Commission, Portugal is among the European countries with the highest number of children affected: 29% of Portuguese children between the ages of 2 and 5 are overweight and 12.5% are obese. In the 6 to 8 age group, the prevalence of overweight is 32% and obesity is 13.9%. Information available at: http://www.apcoi.pt/obesidade-infantil/

189 A study by the World Health Organization, available at http://www.who.int/whr/1998/whr98_ch2.pdf, with forecasts up to 2025 states that cases of lung and colon cancer will continue to rise, largely due to smoking and unhealthy diet, respectively. Another study by the organization, available at http://www.who.int/chp/steps/STEPS_Cameroon.pdf, mentions that in 1997 around 190 million people around the world suffered from diabetes, but that this number will reach 330 million by 2025.

190 See Articles 103 (cigarettes) and 104 (other manufactured tobacco products) of the CIEC. The latter was amended by Law 66-B/2012, of December 31 (LOE 2013), which increased the tax rates.

191 Statistical data for the period 2010 reveal that the standardized mortality rate per Alcohol-related illnesses in Portugal were around 18.1% per 100,000 inhabitants, 32% in men and 5.7% in women. The standardized mortality rate for respiratory diseases per 100,000 inhabitants, also from 2010, was 58.6%, Information from the National Statistics Institute, available at:
http://www.ine.pt/xportal/xmain?xpid=INE&xpgid=ine_indicadores&indOcorrCod=0003786&contexto=bd&selTab=tab2

192 Information available on the website:
http://www.pordata.pt/Portugal/Obitos+for+some+causes+of+death+(percentage)-758

still, through the pricing of goods and services (in which the tax is incorporated)?

First of all, the answer lies in the following question: to what extent are consumer preferences elastic, i.e. does the rise in prices (due to the increase in the tax burden) lead, for example, *drinkers* to switch from alcohol to soft drinks? If the demand for these goods is inelastic, the effect of the tax may lead taxpayers to maintain a *life of sin,* as they forgo the consumption of more worthwhile and healthier goods .[193]

Today, the logic behind taxing alcohol, tobacco and gambling is no longer so much a logic of punishing sinful behaviour, but rather a logic of penalizing risky behaviour. Risky for individual and collective health. Consumers are free to choose their priorities. How can (and/or should) the state interfere in these choices[194] ? Through taxation? Through general consumption tax and excise duties?

The point is that, in our opinion, there are many difficulties in conceiving of VAT as a corrective tax or with corrective purposes, first of all because it is a general tax on consumption. As a general tax, in order to achieve corrective behavior we would have to subdivide it into countless taxes that taxed certain consumptions in isolation. In essence, what we would be doing is creating more excise duties and, in the end, adding to the complexity and administrative costs that we have already mentioned in this study as being avoidable. As far as excise duties are concerned, their main extra-fiscal purpose could be to suppress consumption. Since they are selective in nature, they make it possible to target certain and specific types of consumption with the burden of taxation, thus becoming an alternative to prohibition, without an absolute cost to individual freedom of choice. For example, the taxation of alcohol and alcoholic beverages has a compressive function, for public health reasons; the taxation of cars and fuels has a counter-motivational purpose, for environmental reasons. The Constitution also provides for the correction of negative externalities, as Article 66(h) states that the State is

---

193 Vasques, Sergio, "Os Impostos do Pecado, o Alcool, o Tabaco, o Jogo e o Fisco", Almedina, September 1999.

194 Sergio Vasques, in the work cited, page 216, states that "In a democracy, taxation cannot be based on the maintenance of a paternal state that suppresses the freedom of taxpayers in order to save them the costs of being responsible. Although it is more economical for the state to look after our happiness than for us to do it ourselves, it is not acceptable to suppress individual freedom for reasons of economy"

responsible for "ensuring that fiscal policy makes development compatible with the protection of the environment and quality of life".

Excise duties are intended to compensate in some way for the cost that the consumer taxpayer is presumed to cause the community. It follows that their definition obeys the principle of equivalence, i.e. everyone must pay to the extent of the damage they cause to the community they belong to. If these costs were borne by general taxes, such as VAT, the whole community would be affected and asked to pay. With special taxes, those responsible are called to account, and a requirement of tax equality is met .[195]

---

195 This is why special taxes are called corrective taxes.

7. CONCLUSION

An analysis of the international and national context shows that VAT is a much sought-after tax when it comes to raising revenue. Whether by increasing the standard rate, reducing the number of exemptions or the scope of reduced rates, in recent years many states have made changes to value added tax in order to increase tax revenue.

The choice of indirect taxation is justified as a measure to mitigate the effects of the increase in the tax burden in general (the maintenance/cutting of salaries, rising unemployment rates), insofar as it may be less affected because consumption will always have to exist (although revenues may be reduced as a result of the decrease in consumption).

The question we tried to ask in this study was whether indirect taxation, VAT in particular, could be based on concerns other than raising revenue. Different concerns, but complementary ones, since the very nature of the tax is to raise revenue. The question we asked and debated was, therefore, whether VAT could follow aspirations of shaping taxpayers' behavior, thus influencing the fiscal policy pursued by governments. Whether the tax state can be, at the same time, an educating tax state. If government leaders, when drawing up the guidelines for their organizations, allow themselves to be led by concerns of a distributive, food, environmental, etc. nature. Or whether VAT as a behavioral model wouldn't be somehow unnatural, since the nature of the tax is to collect.

As we have seen, the structure of VAT differs from the outset at EU level, so we can say that there are twenty-eight VAT subsystems. This structure is generally divided into standard rates and reduced rates (the number differs), and may also include a number of exemptions. From the outset, this structure indicates different (but complementary) concerns about raising revenue, since reduced rates and exemptions result in lost tax (i.e. revenue). Note that what we set out to analyze was whether VAT pursues objectives other than raising revenue; not whether it is the best instrument for achieving these objectives.

Opinions are divided on the merits of using reduced rates. The use of reduced rates will always be a political decision, as they will be used as an instrument of fiscal policy. The decision will clearly be motivated by the economic factor. The truth is that this issue is best considered from an economic point of view, namely whether the benefits that may be derived from using reduced rates outweigh the tax losses. Looking at the issue from an economic point of view, in those sectors where reduced rates are currently applied, it is difficult to find convincing economic arguments, based on efficiency or fairness, for maintaining reduced VAT rates. Instead, an economic rationale for making rates more uniform is pointed out, in order to mitigate the distortions arising from differentiated VAT rates. It also points out the administrative problems and compliance costs for businesses and tax authorities that need to be measured and factored into the decision on whether to use reduced VAT rates as a policy tool.

In the national context, the reforms of indirect taxation, and VAT in particular, included the reduction of exemptions and the restructuring of the tax lists annexed to the CIVA. Restructuring which, with a view to avoiding a rise in rates, consisted of transferring categories of goods and services between the different lists and repealing some of them, thus moving to the standard rate of tax. The reform, despite introducing major changes, preserved the application of the reduced tax rate to the *basket of essential goods and services.* The alleged justification for this is to protect the social groups most vulnerable to the impact of the fiscal consolidation measures. At the same time, there is alleged concern for certain sectors of national production, as their goods and products continue to be subject to the intermediate rate.

With regard to the additional revenue generated by the VAT restructuring, it is determined that *"it will be allocated to the financing of the Social Emergency Program, increasing the resources intended to help Portuguese families affected by exclusion and social deprivation".*

So, is VAT structured in such a way as to pursue other objectives than just raising revenue? The structure of a tax with a minimum rate and an intermediate rate, lower than the standard rate, must always be based on reasons other than raising revenue, since it translates into lost revenue. The question that immediately arises is the economic impact of applying reduced rates and, consequently, whether or not reduced VAT rates are an appropriate instrument for achieving sectoral political objectives. The debate on this issue is whether the technical, economic or social reasons on which exemptions and reduced rates are based are still valid and whether the way they are applied can be improved. The debate has implications at the Community level, as individual choices could lead to a conflict between the interests of the Community and those of the member state. There may be cases where extending reduced VAT rates to certain sectors would be economically beneficial for some member states, but could jeopardize the functioning of the internal market.

In a time and context where governments are particularly under pressure to reduce deficits, raising the standard VAT rate has often been seen as an easy and quick measure to increase tax revenues (in some cases temporarily as long as the deficit does not fall to the desired value). However, raising the VAT rate in countries where the rate is already relatively high has some limitations, since when the standard rate is raised and everything else remains the same, the amount of revenue "foregone" due to the application of reduced rates and exemptions also increases. That's why some argue that it might be a better option for governments to consider reforming the *performance of* VAT without necessarily increasing the standard rate. This could include broadening the tax base, limiting the use of reduced rates and exemptions, more efficient tax administration and better compliance.

The question of VAT as a tax that also shapes behavior, we say also because the primary motivation is undeniably to raise revenue, seems to us to be primarily a political decision. The qualification of a good as a merit good is a political decision. And it is for political reasons that it is said that reduced rates or exemptions are very difficult to reverse because they are linked to traditionally benefited sectors, around which there is sometimes a certain emasculation and irrationality in the arguments used for such an advantage. So much so that the decision-makers fear the political consequences of changing these benefits, as they anticipate opposition from those who consider it an affront that the government has only thought of repealing them. There is a kind of untouchable conformation, an *acquired right,* whose possibility of loss is astonishing.

It turns out that political decision-making increasingly listens to economic science and *doesn't decide with its heart.* It depends on its results and evidence. On one side of the balance we have these economic results (which point to the simplification and reduction of benefit systems), while on the other we have social concerns (which point to the use of taxes to realize environmental, technological, demographic, etc. aspirations). Economic science notes that public intervention is necessary, both to overcome market failures and to improve the distribution of income and opportunities that result from the free functioning of markets. However, there may be conflicts between these two objectives and in these cases society, through the political process and thoughtful debate, must consider how much it is willing to sacrifice efficiency in order to achieve equity objectives, or vice versa. In other words, it all comes down to setting priorities and analyzing results, which is closely dependent on who has the power of government at the time.

At the moment, and given the study we have made of the recent changes to value added tax, it seems to us that only very subtle social concerns can be pointed out in these changes. There is an express reference to the need for simplification, to broaden the tax base, to combat tax evasion and fraud (which is allured by complexity), but with a view, it seems to us, to collecting revenue more effectively. The social aspect will lie in maintaining privileged treatment for a range of goods and services, with the most disadvantaged and vulnerable in mind.

Indirect taxation includes excise duties which, in addition to raising revenue, can also discourage the consumption of certain products that are considered harmful. They have therefore been used as a means of influencing consumer behavior in various sectors. The influence will take the form of a disincentive and will be aimed not at momentary results, but at long-term ones (such as improving people's level of health and reducing the number of diagnoses of serious illnesses, with a consequent reduction in public spending on hospitals and health facilities).

In our opinion, there are major difficulties in conceiving of VAT as a corrective tax or with corrective purposes, first and foremost because it is a general tax on consumption. As a general tax, in order to achieve the correction of behavior we would have to subdivide it into countless taxes that tax certain consumptions in isolation. Basically, what we would be doing is creating more excise duties and, in the end, adding to the complexity and administrative costs that we have already mentioned as being avoidable, since the emerging logic is one of simplification.

8. BIBLIOGRAPHY

ANTUNES, BRUNO, *Da Repercussao Fiscal no IVA,* Almedina, 2008

BASTO, XAVIER DE *A Tributagao do Consumo e a sua Coordenação Internacional, Ligoes sobre a Harmonização Fiscal na Comunidade Economica Europeia,* Cadernos de CTF n° 164, Lisbon, 1991

BUYDENS, STEPHANE, CHARLET, ALAIN, *"The OECD's Draft Guidelines on Neutrality for Value Added Taxes,* Taxes Notes International, vol. 61, n. 6, 7.02.2011, 443-448

CHARLET, ALAIN, OWENS, JEFFREY, *"An International Perspective on VAT",* Tax Notes International, N° 12, September 2010, 943-953

EUROPEAN COMMISSION, *Green Paper on the future of VAT: Towards a simpler, stronger and more efficient VAT system,* COM (2010) of 01.12.2010

COMMUNICATION FROM THE COMMISSION TO THE EUROPEAN PARLIAMENT, THE COUNCIL AND THE EUROPEAN ECONOMIC AND SOCIAL COMMITTEE ON THE FUTURE *OF VAT, Towards a simpler, more robust and effective VAT system for the single market,* COM (2011), 06.12.2011.

COMMUNICATION FROM THE COMMISSION TO THE COUNCIL AND THE EUROPEAN PARLIAMENT ON VAT RATES OTHER THAN THE UNIFORM VAT RATES, COM (2007) of 05.07.2007

COPENHAGEN ECONOMICS, *Study on reduced VAT applied to goods and services in the Member States of the European Union,* Final report, dated 21.06.2007, ch. 1-3

COQUIM ANA ISABEL, CAMPELO ANA CATARINA, MARTINS CHRISTINE, BRANDAO SANDRA CRISTINA, RESENDE SUZANNA MARIA, *IVA- Proposta de uma Tributagao Saudavel,* Os 10 Anos de Investigagao do CIJE, Estudos Juridico- Economicos, coordinated by Gloria Teixeira and Ana Sofia Carvalho, Almedina, 2010, 16-42

CRUZ, NEVES JOSE, *Economia e Politica: uma abordagem dialectica da escolha* *pŭbHea,*Coimbra Editora, 2008, 49

EBRILL, V. LIAM, KEEN, MICHAEL, BODIN, JEAN-PAUL and SUMMERS, VICTORIA, *The Modern VAT,* International Monetary Fund, Washington, D.C., 2001.

EUROPEAN COMMISSION, Working Paper N° 2, Mathis Alexandre, *"VAT Indicators",* 2004, 4-12

EUROPEAN COMMISSION, Working Paper N° 32, Kosonen, Katri, *"Regressivity of environmental taxation: myth or reality?"* 2012, 1-19

EUROPEAN COMMISSION, Taxation Paper N° 34, *"Tax Reforms in EU Member States, Tax policy challenges for economic growth and fiscal sustainability",* 2012, 29-119

GO DELFIN S., KEARNEY MARNA, ROBINSON SHERMAN, AND THIERFELDER KAREN, *"An Analysis of South africa's value Added Tax",* World Bank Plocy Research Working Paper N° 3671, 2005, 19

NABAIS, CASALTA *Por um Estado Fiscal Suportavel Estudos de Direito Fiscal,* Almedina, 2008, volume II, chapter 2

OECD (2007), *Consumption Taxes: The Way of the Future",* Policy Brief, OECD Observer, October 2007, 2-7

OECD (2011), *Consumption Tax Trends 2010: VAT/GST and Excise Rates, Trends and Administration Issues*, OECD Publishing, ch. 3 and 5.

OECD (2012), *Consumption Tax Trends 2012: VAT/GST and Excise Rates, Trends and Administration Issues*, OECD Publishing, ch. 1, 3 and 5.

OWENS J., BATTIAU, P. AND CHARLET A. (2011), *"VAT's next half century: Towards a single-rate system?",* OECD Observer 284, 23-24

PALMA, CLOTILDE CELORICO:

"The Commission's Recent Communication on the Future of VAT", Revista TOC n° 144, March 2012, 48-55

"The VAT Reform - some proposals", TOC Magazine No. 135, July 2011, 2628

"A Harmonizagdo comunitaria do Imposto sobre o Valor Acrescentado: Quo

Vadis?", Revista de Ciencias Empresariais e Juridicas, No. 5, September 2005, Separata.

Introduction to Value Added Tax, 5ª edigao, Almedina, 2011

The Green Paper on the Future of VAT - Some Reflections, Revista de Finangas Publicas e de Direito Fiscal, Year IV, No. 1, March 2011.

PEREIRA, PAULO TRIGO; AFONSO, ANTONIO; ARCANJO, MANUELA; SANTOS, JOSE, *Economia e Finangas Phblicas,* Escolar Editora, 2nd Edition, 2006, 71-74

SAMUELSON/NORDHAUS, *Economia,* copy of the original *Economics,* 16th edition, McGraw Hill de Portugal, Lda., 1999, 394

SANCHES, SALDANHA, *Manual de Direito Fiscal,* 3rd edition, Coimbra Editora, 2007

SANTOS, ANTONIO CARLOS DOS, *The European common VAT system: merits, difficulties and perspectives of evolution,* Revista de Finangas Publicas e Direito Fiscal, n° 3, Ano I, Almedina, 2008.

TAIT, ALAN, *Value Added Tax: International Practice and Problems,* International Monetary Fund, 1988, ch. 3 and 4

TEIXEIRA, GLORIA *Manual de Direito Fiscal,* 2nd edition, Almedina, 2010, ch. 3

VASQUES, SERGIO, *"Origem e Finalidades dos Impostos Especiais de Consumo",* RFDT, Belo Horizonte, year 3, n° 17, 2005, 49-98

VASQUES, SERGIO, *Os Impostos do pecado, O Alcool, o Tabaco, o Jogo e o Fisco,* Almedina, 1999, ch. 3

WORLD COMMERCE REVIEW, *Improving Performance of VAT Systems,* September 2011, volume 5, 8-10

SITIOS CONSULTADOS: http://info.portaldasfinancas.gov.pt/NR/rdonlyres/655D2CB7-C79E-478B-987A- EA4F9780EFAE/0/INFORMA%C3%87%C3%83O.1083.pdf, consultada em 22.04.2012 http://info.portaldasfinancas.gov.pt/NR/rdonlyres/48AFBC2E-521B-460C-BBF7- 44FF2F8F77A0/0/INFORMA%C3%87%C3%83O.1276.pdf 22.04.12

http://info.portaldasfinancas.gov.pt/NR/rdonlyres/84B15603-D008-404E-A7A4-67C914DF63E9/0/INFORMA%C3%87%C3%83O.1028.pdf http://www.who.int/whr/1998/media center/50facts/en/, visited on 19.04.2013 http://www.who.int/whr/1998/whr98 ch2.pdf, visited on 19.04.2013 http://ec.europa.eu/portugal/temas/ajuda economica portugal/index pt.htmvisited on 23.04.13 http://www.ine.pt/xportal/xmain?xpid=INE&xpgid=ine indicadores&indOcorrCod=0005021&cont exto=bd&selTab=tab2visited on 20.05.2013 http://www.ine.pt/xportal/xmain?xpid=INE&xpgid=ine indicadores&indOcorrCod=0003786&cont exto=bd&selTab=tab2visited on 20.05.13 http://www.apcoi.pt/obesidade-infantil/visitada on 21.05.13

http://www.pordata.pt/Portugal/Obitos+por+al+causas+de+morte+(percentagem)-758visited on 21.05.13 http://www.ine.pt/xportal/xmain?xpid=INE&xpgid=ine idsustentavel&contexto=es&selTab=tab0&INST=123716083visited on 22.05.13

http://issuu.com/oecdobserver/docs/284q12011.

http://skatteverket. se/ omskatteverket/rapporter.4.584dfe 11039cdb626980000.html

Buy your books fast and straightforward online - at one of world's fastest growing online book stores! Environmentally sound due to Print-on-Demand technologies.

Buy your books online at
www.morebooks.shop

Kaufen Sie Ihre Bücher schnell und unkompliziert online – auf einer der am schnellsten wachsenden Buchhandelsplattformen weltweit! Dank Print-On-Demand umwelt- und ressourcenschonend produziert.

Bücher schneller online kaufen
www.morebooks.shop

Printed by Books on Demand GmbH, Norderstedt / Germany